THE PASSION OF PHINEAS GAGE &
SELECTED POEMS

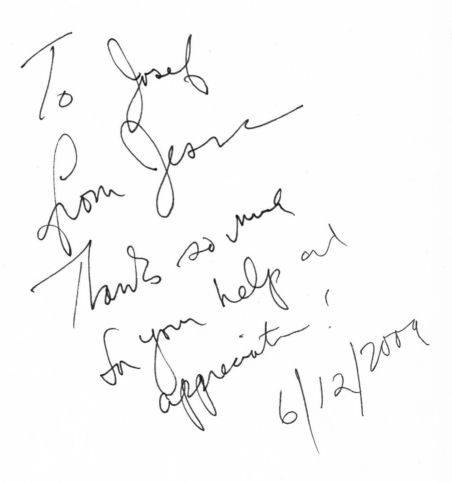

To Josef
from Jesma
Thanks so much
for your help and
appreciate !
6/12/2009

THE PASSION OF PHINEAS GAGE &
SELECTED POEMS

JESSE GLASS

West House & *aha*dada
Books **books**
sheffield · toronto · tokyo

West House Books & Ahadada Books gratefully acknowledges the support of the Foreign Languages Department of Meikai University, Shin-Urayasu, Japan, in the production of this book.

First Edition
Printed and bound in Canada

editorial addresses:

West House Books
40 Crescent Rd
Sheffield S7 1HN
United Kingdom

3158 Bentworth Drive
Burlington, Ontario
Canada L7M-1M2

Meikai University
8 Akemi, Urayasu-shi
Chiba-ken, Japan 279-8550

National Library of Canada Cataloguing in Publication

Glass, Jesse

The passion of Phineas Gage & selected poems / Jesse Glass.

ISBN 0-9732233-8-3 (Ahadada Books).—ISBN 1-904052-18-5 (West House Books)

I. Title.

PS3557.L298P38 2005   811'.54   C2005-907074-9

Table of Contents

Acknowledgments

Thanks to Alan Halsey of West House Books, Marvin Sackner of the Ruth and Marvin Sackner Archive of Visual Poetry, Jared Pierce, Dan Sargent, John Solt and Jerome Rothenberg for suggestions regarding the contents of this volume, Dan Sendecki for fearlessly facing down the forces of entropy and Del, Nancy, Katie, Rod, Tom, Derek, Korin, Kolin, Ethan, Kathleen, Maya, Delmar Yoichi and Junko Tennessee for picking up the pieces. A further thanks to the editors and proprietors of the books, magazines, anthologies and websites that have featured versions of these poems over the years. "Lecturing on Walt Whitman and Emily Dickinson in China" first appeared in *Visiting Walt* from the University of Iowa Press in 2003. "Against the Agony of Matter" features in the soundtrack of *Faites vos Jeux* by Filmgruppe Chaos (2003). Inspired versions of "Puppet Psalms" and "Mayakovsky is Dead" were recorded in 2002 by the Dutch performance artist Charles Krutzen. "The Passion of Phineas Gage" appeared in Lou Rowan's *Golden Handcuffs* for summer/fall 2005, and in a limited edition from Road to Excess Books.

Cover art: "Apocalyptic Beast" by Jesse Glass (2002), private collection, Nagasaki, Japan.

The Passion of Phineas Gage

1.

On September 13th, 1848, 25-year-old Phineas P. Gage was transformed in an instant from a responsible foreman for the Rutland and Burlington Railroad in New England to a profane, social outcast who could no longer abide life as husband and father. The medium of this remarkable change was an iron tamping bar 3 cm. thick and 109 cm. long that was sent rocketing through Gage's brain in a bizarre accident with black powder. Gage that day was involved in blasting rock. First a hole was drilled in stone, then black powder was poured in the hole and a layer of fine sand poured above the black powder before the explosive was tamped into place with an iron bar. On the day in question, Gage, busied in conversation, did not check to see if his assistant had poured the sand above the charge and proceeded to tamp directly into the powder. The resulting explosion stunned, but did not kill him. Remarkably, Gage lived another 12 years after his transfiguration, but the accident seemed to have deprived him of all moral sense. He became a drifter, working as temporary help on farms and in freak shows. He seems to have had a special affinity for horses and a mania for collecting. He worked as a coach driver in Chile—enjoying a brief return to normalcy—had a relapse and returned to his family in the U.S. When he died in 1860 he was buried with the bar that had changed his life.

.

The text for the body of the "bar" is taken from the inscription on the bar itself as quoted in Malcolm Macmillan's excellent *An Odd Kind of Fame* (M.I.T. Press, 2002.) The exhibits are from Descartes' *The Passions of the Soul*, Elizabeth S. Haldane translation. (Chicago: Great Books Foundation, 1960.) Quotations from Harlow and Freeman are from original publications by Harlow and Bigelow as cited in Macmillan. Finally, Malcolm Macmillan answered my query concerning Gage's marital status by indicating that, factually, it is not known if he had a wife and family; poetically we say he did. He also assured us that this is the only long poem to treat of this subject. *Jesse Glass 1/20/2004.*

2.

Dr. J.M. Harlow to the Boston Medical and Surgical Journal

Dear Sir,—Having been interested in the reading of the cases of "injuries of the Head," reported in your Journal by Professor Shipman of Courtlandville, N.Y., I am induced to offer you the notes of a very severe, singular, and, so far as the result is taken into account, hitherto unparalleled case, of that class of injuries, which has recently fallen under my own care. The accident happened in this town, upon the line of the Rutland and Burlington Rail Road, on the 13th of Sept., last, at 4 ½ o'clock, P.M. [1848]. The subject of it is Phineas P. Gage, a foreman, engaged in building the road, 25 years of age, of middle stature, vigorous physical organization, temperate habits, and possessed of considerable energy of character....

The tamping rod is round, and rendered comparatively smooth by use. It is pointed at the end which entered first, and is three feet, seven inches in length, one and one quarter inch in diameter, and weighs 13 1/4 pounds. I am informed that the patient was thrown upon his back, and gave a few convulsive motions of his extremities, but spoke in a few minutes. His men (with whom he was a great favorite) took him in their arms and carried him to the road, only a few rods distant, and sat him into an ox cart, in which he rode, sitting erect, full three quarters of a mile, to the hotel of Mr. Joseph Adams, in this village. He got out of the cart himself, and with a little assistance walked up a long flight of stairs, into the hall, where he was dressed.

3.

Aaron's Rod

The, bolt, that, stove, my, left,
cheek, &, breached, the, top, of, my, skull,
was, a, Watcher's, tower, forged, of, Aaron's, iron.
Blank, angel, faces, skewed, my, muscled, history,
the, way, of, Caw * Caw * crows, &, surging, horses, &, those,
low, creeping, ridge-back, things, under, rocks,
tinked-One-Er-Two-by, a, 10 lb., railroad, hammer, &, you,
could, see, another, image, of, God's, gone,
down, on, his, whorly, knuckles, boyz.

All, things, gazed, upon, me,
from, towering, wings, &, legs,
as, it, struck, thunderbolt,
risen, (mysterious E), from, the, stone,
&, witnessed, &, writ, of, by, Benjamin, Frank, I, bet,
or, some, such, patriot.

&, I, fell, upon,
my, kneez,

Jesus, Apocalypsis,

driven, deep,
into, the, greenback, mud,
&, part, of, me, way, up, in, the, banner-like, clouds,
unfurling, my, secret, history,
to, all, &, sundry, of, Vermont,

&, I, couldn't, swallow,
boyz,

their, shouts, their, familiar, names,
their, chill, dipper, held, to, my, twitch,
as, it, all, went, up, like, a, 4th, of, July, rocket,

dressed, in, fire, &, blood,
        up, up, to, the, Alamo, sun.
God, O,
O, GOOOOOOOO
D   Think, I, said,
        &, someone's, crying, holding,
a, rag, to, my, head, saying,
keep, still/ he's, alive.

            &, I, should, have, died,
&, did, die,
alone,
&, came, back, ANOTHER, howdy, fella,
        damn.

4.

From Dr. J. M. Harlow's Diary.

14th, 7 A.M.—Has slept some; appears to be in pain; speaks with difficulty; tumefaction of face considerable, and increasing; pulse 70; knows his friends, and is rational. Asks who is foreman in his pit. Hemorrhage internally continues slightly. Has not vomited since 12 A.M.

5.

What I can Recall

   is, someone, called, my, name,
&, it, didn't, blind, me,

I, can, yet, see,

   bullet, hole,
   in, cellar, door,
   down, Klinamen, street,

taste,
   copper,   copper, sure,
tongue, loop, out,
lolling, lapping,
   sweat, of, wife's, thigh,

feel,
   hummingbird's, hard, spiral,
   though, left, hand's,
a, bit, numb,   e'en, clinkered, &,
Lord,
   felt, a, lightning, flash,
      (Elijah,
    dragged, me,
  instant, brow, to, cloud,
  golden, mask, knocked, awry,

   golden, wafer, laughing, in, my, eye,

before, I, began,

stepping, these, high, sevens,
that, was, tin, to, copper, ago,

when, everyone, stopped, chewing,
I, was,
the, GREAT, MAN,

bent, behind, the, granite,
forehead,
lighting, the, all-mighty, FUSE,

&, it, didn't, hurt, boyz,
JUST, KEEP, AWAY, THE, FLIES,

Doctor, stepping, round, me,
touching, this, packing, that, with,

cotton, &, long, nippers. Carbolic,
like, pig's, breath, larding, my, nostrils,

hands,
tied, to, the, bedsides,
so, they, don't, crawl, away,

&, I ain't, yr., idiot, yet,
2 + 2. See? The, Capitol,
of, these, United, States, is, etc.,

&, Taylor's, our, great, &c., And, the, time, right, now,
by, the, STATION, CLOCK, is, no, epitaph,
for, a, hardy, son, of, Jefferson,
who, still, chews, with, the, best, of, 'em,
&, spits, just, as, pretty.

6.

...I went to the place where the accident happened. I found upon the rocks, where I supposed he had fallen, a small quantity of brains. There being no person at this place, I passed on to a blacksmith's shop a few rods beyond, in and about which a number of Irishmen were collected. As I came up to them, they pointed me to the iron, which has since attracted so much attention, standing outside the shop door. They said they found it covered with brains and dirt, and had washed it in the brook. The appearance of the iron corresponded with this story. It has a greasy appearance, and was so to the touch....

—Joseph Freeman

7.

From Dr. J.M. Harlow's Diary

18th, 9 A.M.—Slept well all night, and lies upon his right side. Pulse 72; tongue red and dry; breath foetid. Removed the dressings, and passed a probe to the base of the cranium without giving pain. Patient says he shall recover. He is delirious, with lucid intervals.

Oct. 11th.—Pulse 72. Intellectual faculties brightening. When I asked him how long since he was injured, he replied, "four weeks this afternoon at 4 ½ o'clock." Relates the manner in which it occurred, and how he came to the house. He keeps the day of the week and time of day, in his mind. Says he knows more than half of those who inquire after him. Does not estimate size or money accurately, though he has memory as perfect as ever. He would not take $1000 for a few pebbles which he took from an ancient river bed where he was at work.

20th.—Improving. Gets out and into bed with but little assistance. Sits up thirty minutes twice in twenty-four hours. Is very childish; wishes to go home to Lebanon, N.H. The wound in the scalp is healing rapidly.

Nov. 5th.—I learn, on inquiry, that Gage has been in the street every day except Sunday, during my absence. His desire to be out and to go home to Lebanon has been uncontrollable by his friends, and he has been making arrangements to that effect. Yesterday he walked half a mile, and purchased some small articles at the store.

17th.—Improving. Expresses himself as 'feeling better in every respect;' has no pain in the head.

Exhibit 1.

Of the origin of tears.

As laughter is never caused by the greatest joys, so tears do not proceed from an extreme sadness but only from that which is moderate and accompanied or followed by some feeling of love or likewise of joy. And in order to understand their origin properly, we must remark that although a mass of vapors continually escape from all the portions of our body, there are at the same time none from which so much issues as the eyes, because of the size of the optic nerves and the multitude of little arteries by which the vapors reach them; and as the sweat is simply composed of vapors which, issuing from the other parts of the body, are converted into water on their surface, so tears are formed from the vapors which issue from the eyes.

8.

Mrs. Gage Recollects

He come home alright. Rose like a specter before us scratching the bar on the door to be let in. He'd walked all the way & stood proud (it seemed) & even grinning, though he'd stopped once or twice to vomit in the grass. The boys stood in the yard despairing over their friend and work-mate. They'd collected among them half a year's wages & passed the money to me in secret. Good souls. They took their leave & promised to return to see us. Several did, to their regret, later.

Laughed at their concern & laid down in the parlor, singing a lewd song. I placed cold wraps on his red & peeling brow. "No pain," he said, and moaned. "The smell of honey...biscuits..." he said, but couldn't finish. Coughed up more charnel stuff. Those biscuits, do you want 'em? I asked. He sighed...then laughing...called for ale. I thought how strange. My Phineas was no drinker in his own home. "This is no tavern," I told him, "but we have plenty cold water." Then he pursed his fevered lips for my kiss. And when I bent and kissed him he thrust his tongue in my mouth & the taste was of no living man, but I showed my fortitude for I loved him well, and staid till he released me. Backed away from his raven's gasp laughter.

"Bring the children, Marnie." I did. And a dipper of water. He placed his hand on Billy's head while Faith, the younger, stood tear-eyed by the door. "Does it hurt much, Papa?" "Naw," he says to Bill. "I am a struck rock gushing laughter! Hear?" How odd that he began that shrill, unnecessary laughter. "Won't you rest?" I asked. "Now hungry! Hungry! Woman?" As if I didn't know the language he spoke. He even gestured as the deaf do to explain. I brought soup broth. Baked his biscuits. Faith helped. He ate only a little like an actor in a play, rolling his eyes the while. Then bent gagging into his hand. The children were fearful. They tried not to stare overmuch at his shattered head; the visible pulse of his brain.

The hateful rod that changed him would not come clean no matter how I scrubbed it with brush and lye-salts. "We'll hang it over the fireplace...an aid for meditation. Better than a bust of Washington! Take down Grand-daddy's musket!" He directed it in place upon the screws in a foreman's harshest voice.

The preacher came, but Gage would have no prayers said, no hymns sung, in his presence. "I've forgotten gods & angels. That rod left a steel egg buried in my head & it hatches dragons, minister. Can you slay 'em?" The preacher grinned like wood and never called again.

I opened the window daily, for the smell of his sick room was of the battlefield. He dandled the rod in his arms, crooning sometimes—a parody of mothers.

But it was when I found him with Faith in the woodshed, her frock pulled up and she looking far off at the mountains and he with strap in hand ready to lay on like a skinner that I pushed that grub of a man out, still hooting laughter like an owl, winking his one good, tear-filled eye. Gave him half his wages, an overcoat, the bar.

He came back once or twice to beg some scraps of food and steal some petty things from the boy. And then was gone, what was, I'm sad to say, once a good man and my husband.

Exhibit 2.

This is the bar that was shot thru the head of Mr. Phin. P. Gage at Cavendish, VT. Sept. 14, 1848. He fully recovered from the injury & deposited this bar in the Museum of the Medical College, Harvard University. Phin. P Gage Jan 6 1850.

"It was subsequently reclaimed by the patient."

Exhibit 3.

Laughter consists in the fact that the blood, which proceeds from the right orifice in the heart by the arterial vein, inflating the lungs suddenly and repeatedly, causes the air which they contain to be constrained to pass out from them with an impetus of the windpipe, where it forms an inarticulate and explosive utterance; and the lungs in expanding equally with the air as it rushes out, set in motion all the muscles of the diaphragm from the chest to the neck, by which means they cause motion in the facial muscles, which have a certain connection with them.

9.

Dr. Harlow

He took to travelling, and visited Boston, most of the large New England towns, and New York, remaining awhile in the latter place at Barnum's, with his iron.

10.

Step This Way!

Coofer, the, Gibble, Boy,
sits, opposite,
smoking, all, de, carefree, day,...

hums, now, &, then, your, Stephen, Foster, ditty,
Lucky, Coof!

I, chew, a, shard, of, jerky,
sweat, in, my, crepe,
gentleman's, outfit, (fake, as, Barnum's, scruples,)   then, strain,
my, doodah, brain, right, up,

against, the, breach, (Owen, Monster, heaving,
in, the, wallows,)
            in, time, for, abridged, Napoleons,
        to, adjust, their, banter,

&, sing, along, come, along,
to, Coof's, camptown, racers,
work, your, turkey, gorges, large, &, small!
Then, I, stow, the, squeeze-box, &,
strike, the, spit-on, sawdust, floor,

my, rod, a, Tammany, King's,
&, lay, 'em, out, some,
sermonal, expectorations,   Send, 'em,

tumbling, hands, over, ears,
hands, over, their, kiddies', ears,
wife-blush-daughter-vile, sententious, dippy-doodle,
the, price—I say—the, price, of, gawking,

like, when, I, fawt,
&, scatter, da, sooty, pigeons, in, da, pawk.

A, tough, gets, mad, &, squalls, to, trim, my, hash,
 I, haw, haw,
&, Coof, howls,
blinks, like, a, sour-milk, ghost, (razor, flashing,
underz, tongue,)

Kid, backs, away,
        We, sing, &, fling, our, bile!
doodling, our, boodles,
bibbling, our, bullies,
&,
        they,
                surely,
                        dis-

                                em,

                                        bark,
divining, the, egress, like, a, turpentined, hound,
backpaws, up, and, a**hole, kissing, terra....

All, the, way,
to, their, uptown, cribs.

Oy!,
Fat, Girl, &, Johnny, Twist,
Rubber, Face, &, Chicken, Baby,
(those, that, taste, not, death,)
want, me, gone,

I, tend, to, agree,

Old, Barnum, buys, me, white, shirt, fronts,
&, sez, I, owe, him,   what?
C. Baby's, egg, kiss, most, midnights?
Love, for, an, old, Freak-man?

Cat, head, with, eyes: Coof-boy,
lit, punk, in, the, dark,

moans, Momma, Momma, &, his,
red, gums,   bleed,
stuff, what, flies, eat,

Coughs, right, in, yr., Metrotonic, face,
the, gooh—but, I, forgive, him/
we, own, the, self-same, cardboard, star,
&, crib. Trippers. Askers. Barnum's, buskers.

We, shake, our, tambourines,
for, tokens,
before, the, poster, that, makes, my, head,
look, like, Bald Mountain, spouting, blood,
(or, is, it, a, Nantucket, oil, well,
gushing, ambergris?)
my, face, a, pimpled, question,
but, I've, my, plan, writ, large,
on, toothy, paper,
stuck, in, my, hatband...

Can, youse, read, by, phospher, match?
Meet, me, heyah, dis, midnight, noon.

Exhibit 4.

And then the lungs are also sometimes inflated suddenly by the abundance of the blood which enters them, and which drives out from them the air which they contained, which, issuing by the windpipe, begets the groans and cries which usually accompany tears.

11.

Nimrod Gardner Recollects

I'd known some like
him before: obvious liar; Indian fighter

he says; candidate for work house/unmarked grave

& who, looking
at him could trust one pismire utterance

of this gravel-throated nondescript
hat on head & always rain-stained hat

beneath a buttermilk sky &
always sweat rotting his

shirt pits & a smell
that draws flies, but lookit he says

lookit & he trembles the yellowed
newspaper clip into your palm

& you're almost afraid to touch
it like a flake of Paddy's skin

or bad breath made visible
curling, crumbling as you read; he

grins black teeth. You find the one
truth about him: note the scarred cheek, stitched socket

jaw knocked out of plumb
& Understand the whisper; the scarecrow hat above

the stitched-up flap of scalp:
but the eyes (see 'em), monkey-like

taking in everything around as if searching
for a tool to break a strong box

& the hands moving among boxes, keys, coins
weighing, sifting, touching the textures

Was married he says. Where's she? Vermont.
& Kids? Had 'em. See the grin, back hand gobbing

at the nose. Been drinking hard? Not overmuch.
Where you work last? Farming help. Ever been in jail?
Nope. (But see the eyes!) I'll think about it, and he's

squinting up at the loft like he means to linger. Can't stay here, I say.
Come back
when hell freezes over.

12.

Dr. Harlow

In August, 1852, nearly four years after his injury, he turned his back upon New England, never to return....

13.

By train **By wagon** **By thumb**

out, again, under, a, freckle-belly-of-a-mackerel-cloud,
a, horizon, of, burning, crowns/
fallen, Watchers',
umber, recursions: There's, Samael,
&, grinning, Ock,

I, lag, along, to, name, them, all,

in, Ohio, climbed, up, an, Injun, Earth, Snake,
eating, Dirt, Egg, &, slept, a, night, on, it,   ate, a, robin's,
raw, egg,   too,   torn, from, the, nest, then,

Had, a, funny, dream, of, Hell,
chisels, striking, stone, so, you, felt, it,
in, tooth, throat, &, chest, (ivied, yard, of, dim, ascenders,)
saying, Born, (   ) Died, (   )
till, time, bought,
rest, there, as, a, tied-together, mesh, of, bones, pickt, clean of, ashes.
          Came, a, fair, morning

&, I, awoke, to, speculate, a, bit, on, the, spider,
throned, on, my, pack, in, evaporating, dew,
enjoying, heat, &, connection,   thorn-babies,
clutching, her, belly,   all, gem-like,
Wheel, within, Wheel, within, Wheel,

when, I, stirred, she, drizzled, down, a, thread,
taking, her, future, with, her,   &, I, walked,
into, bird, laughter, following, the, South,
eating, &, sleeping, where, I, would, &, could,
until, I, wantoned, in, a, desert,
full, of, mica, &, slack, steel,   gut,
shriveled, like, my, thing,brain, dished, down,
into, skull, as, a, badger, hunkers, in, a, wind-bunkered, burrow,

lips, receding, eyelids, caving, in,
I, searched, a, map, for, death, &, said,   ok,

Came, a, wagon,   jingle,   wheel, ruts, filled, with, bouncing, wood,
rolling,   felloes, shadows,   old, man, woman,
&, a, slab-footed, mule,   stumble,
Hauled, me, up, &, in,   Mud, Mother, Dust, Daddy,
clay, scab, of, a, home,   civil, Cherokees,   they, jabbered,
leaned, me, in, a, corner,   thru, sacking, curtains, saw, black, snakes, raced,
across, the, level,   trackless, trains,   full, throttle,

&, One, above, the, clouds,   ached, along, I, finger-roofed, my,eyes, &, saw,
dust, devils, prance, beneath, it,
pulverizing, sand,   my, head, unsteady, in, a, grid, of, pork, grease, smoke,
turned, to, Crystal,   afternoon,   Mule, slobbered, his, oats,
a, snake, drank, from, a, puddle,   color, of, whiskey,
I, stood, &, walked, unsteady, toward, the, flies,
huddled, on, a, copper, hand, that, pointed, Where (?)...Then, saw,
among, the, eagle-crowned, cacti,
a, reedy, Head, of, Black, Clay, lips, working,
                    cool, vowels,
water, dribbling, from, chin, a, spring, of, green, water, welling, from, each, eye,
          &, the, nose, a, broken, clam, &, the, fuming, hair, the, color,
                    of, the, moon, at, dawn/called, me, brother,
                              &, taught, me,
                    songs, of, those, who, have, lost,
                                        thing,
                              after,
                                        thing,
                              after,
                              fly-blown, thing,
                    (as, per, limited, me:
                    the, eye, in, the, needle,
                    thru, which, starlight, does, not, slow,

                    before, it, drills, &, drills, the, dust.

14.

Hooah!

My wide-brimmed Mexican Cowboy Hat & Cape!
Who would have thought it?
and two leather lines of three sweet horses each
pulling us up and down the dusty curves of Valparaiso!

Long cross-piece I could even walk on full-a-gallop
if I wanted to flex myself before a perfumed stranger,
but choose not to. Just sun-burnt heaven is all—
up here figuring the road in dark of half-a-brain!

Even fares. Can make change as fast as I make water.
Lady, yr. ticket costs one half a dollar U.S. Let Diego weigh
that trunk before we heft it up. Yep, the weather's not half bad
now is it? That's five cents extra charges for the strap.

Got me a seniorita sit across my hips
& don't pay nothin' for the pleasure! At night I sleep
in a room next to the horses and polish
the Concord coach on my off days. See here

how I pop the moths from the sky
with my snake-hide whip? Who
would have thought these hands
this face, these skills would now be ma-ma-mine?
A man with half-a-brain could live forever!

15.

Jonathan Golly

Steady worker, old Phin-Boy
but his health grew weak

and it was that bitch woman
spooned him rot-gut whiskey so much

in the alley cantinas;

it hurt to watch him drink
like a monkey trained to the glass—

stutters and twitches
& mumbles
and shitting himself and stealing

from my tools too. The woman run
off with whatever pesos he had

(sad story older
than dust)

and we found him
not eating nor drinking for days, but

staring staring staring
at his hands.

16.

Gage Shows His Collection

Treasures, aplenty, in, this, here, box:
A, Spanish, bit, eat, near, in, 2, by, rust,
        a, mossy, stone, pict,
up, on, the, pampas. Mohawk-bristle-rat-skull,
        lacks, one, bookish, comment, old perfesser,
(which, I, call, him,)
A, whip, with,
        a, snake-headed, handle, here.
Arrowhead. Bola, Bola. Wedding, ring. Ticket,
        stubs, from, pop, Barnum's,
disaster. Some, paper, dolls,
        cut, by, brujos, Valparaiso, way.
One, broken, locket, with, a, sunbit, beat,
        tintype, inside, (I'll,
not, show, you, it, no.) Silver,
        watch, less, minute, hand. A,
dried-up, sparrow, eat,
        hollow, by, ants. Mex.,
Doll, of, fired, clay, agrin, &, several, size,
        of, pens, pins, &, drawing,
chalks, taken, from, the, dresser,
        of, a, boy, (Guess, whose,) I, left,
asleep, one, cheery,
        Thursday, morning. (Never,
went, back. He's, asking, yet, where's, Pa, I, bet.)
        French, playing, cards.
Lookit. Two, women, kissing. Vote,
        for, Lincoln, hankie.
A, good, carved, pipe,
&, a, funny, stone,
        hold, to, my, eye,
        &, the, world's, turnt,
upside, down,
        for, as, long, as, you, can, stand,
the, squint.
Want, to, see?

17.

My Poor Son Returned

face twisted scratched & dirty
hooked nails
he's a sad wild thing
eating uncooked potatoes
from the field

foul, foul, needs
an enfant's clout
            ribs pumping
under blue skin, each
eyeball a baby bird's veiny
capsule of sight. "Maw"
he can barely say—big as
a twelve year old boy
with the stumbling rickets—then he's
raving off into Spanish or some
other lingo he picked up
like the Bad Disease down south
in heathen civilization. His scabby
body does a dance
when he's not looking—
like each toy muscle's set on fire
by electrical machines.
            "Come here, poor Phin.,
Poor Phiney-boy, Maw's
Phiney-Boy—
Rest yourself, child. The world's
done you a terrible turn," his
hat of rotten rags on his head,
which I peel off with my
fingernails, so the moonlight
shines on the brain
wallowing beneath a flexible weight of scars.
& he's crying,

sucking the hem of my dress
doubled over on the floor
by the weight of the distances
he's crossed to find me.

legs & arms doing a horrid
half twist of a dance
even when he's a-bed.

18.

"Baby" Os Shattuck

And then he'd gone down to the bottom of the sea in one of them hard-hat suits and lightning struck the air-pumpers up on the deck, but he warn't afraid because he knew all he had to do was hold his breath kick off his boots and hard hat and scramble up to the boat using his secret indian method of swimming taught him by Naked Fellow, who was his best indian buddy after rescuing him when he was 3/4s scalped out discovering californy in the gold rush. i said uncle phin you tells the best stories and he tells me go fuck myself, but that's just unc. phin when he's feeling low and twitchy. he says he had to bunk down in a haunted house onct but found out the ghost was nothing but a mouse pushing acorns down the stairs with its nose, and says he found some pirate treasure in vermont where the best men and women in the world live not like this san francisco place with earthquakes and fog and all—and about that pirate treasure he buried it out in the jakes so why don't i go dig for it there? And turns over and twitches some more.

19.

Dr. Harlow:

At 5 o'clock, A.M., on the 20th, he had a severe convulsion. The family physician was called in, and bled him. The convulsions were repeated frequently during the succeeding day and night, and he expired at 10 P.M., May 21, 1860.

20.

C.S. Stauffer, Sexton, Laurel Hill Cemetery

By order of great WOOLY HEADS
back East, we drag the iron
Fisk case to the surface &
wrestle it among the picks & spades
onto the cemetery grass.
A miserable steady rainy day
& I have a hell of a cold. "Go on,"
I say

& they work the bolts free
on the face plate & we peer down
into the wild wolf hair-half-obscured
leather glove Physog. of said subject:
the lips a tan snarl above
black teeth.

"That's him" the in-law says,
"old Phin-boy." Phin who? They crack
the seal & air whooshes in
so the case pings & slams

& we prize open its putrid gaskets & puzzle its
rusted hinges apart. The doctor
kneels with saw and scalpel
his elbow pumping above a moldy blue suit
obliquely glimpsed (who would want
to look at it?)

& puts what he came for in a box
and the box into a scarlet, draw-string bag.
Also takes up
an iron rod some workman
forgot in the box! (What kind of
worker was so forgetful
as that? No doubt a drifter.)

We claim our fee & the doctor
tells us—"We'll render him down
light, pure & cleansed
of all ideas,
then matriculate him at Harvard
to delight the pinz-nez Brahmins."

Five dollars to me
and two to the diggers each.
The in-law wants to stand us
for a drink, and we'll oblige him.

All but the doctor, that is
who's in a great hurry
to attend the San Francisco Doctors'
charity luncheon. He's run off
with box, bag and maggoty tool
through the winter rain!

21.

Dr. Harlow

I desire here to express gratefully my obligations, and those of the Profession, to D.D. Shattuck, Esq., brother-in-law of the deceased; to Dr. Coon, Mayor of San Francisco, and to Dr. J. D. B. Stillman, for their kind cooperation in executing my plans for obtaining the head and tamping iron, and for their fidelity in personally superintending the opening of the grave and forwarding what we so much desired to see.

22.

Gage's Song

Then lean me against a wall,
an extravagant clock of bone
my hands counter-weighting my skull
(a bowler hat on a stick)
   The dial reading 0 & 0.

My pecker sharp as a thorn
has crumbled as the rose,
my ribs encumber the sky
—sun-leached ties in rows—
my absence clatters down
   upon the indifferent town.

Though muscles stripped and parched
can never shift my weight
to caper before your God
singing to tabor and harp—
   I am your athlete.

23.

(His Transfiguration):

The Tamping Rod Is Round & Rendered Comparatively Smooth By Use

PHINEAS

Color of railroads

Appears to be in pain. Note the radiant tongue.
(golden aurora)
Hummingbird's hard spiral,
that was tin to copper ago
alone ALONE

he got into the cart himself

The Color of

    S,E,E?

cotton & long nippers

keep away the cuckoo eggs

sez—(rowing motion & a short jerking up signals spinal damage)

ONE CUTS WITH A KNIFE

What! Harmonies of flies corrode the weeping manual. The slipper-shaped bag of protoplasm erupts a dart.

ONE SEWS WITH A NEEDLE

There is not that single thing which is doubled in a moment. Or maybe a butterfly's wings do indeed decflocculate a fossil ruler long without a name. But we are too humble to discuss the ultimate with such short notice.

ONE WHISTLES WITH A WHISTLE

Fire appears hot and water fluid upon the application of inert earths and cupping glasses to an origami swan. Do you follow the argument? we asked him. No, but I see a future of frontier journeys up mountains surrounded by dark or hairy men.

ONE SAWS WITH A SAW

Know? No, it is impossible you or any man alive should know it. All you know is a preponderance of negative electrons whose tenuous bonds give way before a sugar-coated rim.

ONE DIGS WITH A SPADE

It is.

ONE PLAYS WITH A TOY

They have none of them anything of themselves, of those real things or anything like them in gold in tree in stone. Must all have no absolute existence really in gold? They are only relative to our senses, and we are all diminished to the size of honeybees in ciphers.

20th—Is very childish; dry fetid breath.

19th—Monosyllables. Ordered a cathartic.

11th—$1000.00 for a few worthless pebbles.

The hateful rod war flesh-sloggered screws along a fireplace. Hock. Smell was terrible
                                                                                    passed a probe
chamber brain right up 12:45 up feathers of a yellow bird up   wired wrist
                                                                                    lifted weighe/d
                                                                                    ceiling

pose of man of horse of dog
justified with formalin—
                    rod a king's
abridged Napoleon, debunk   Turner or race horse splatter Tongue
injected wax to keep organic form tenable
(Carlos Wms.)

                    rod a king's
          heft buckets o' mirrors skyward
begin the awkward music of breaking

               burrs of inverted light
in morning lens:

smell of broken mirrors

I NEVER SAW THIS MOVEMENT BEFORE.

girl's eyelash weathers on her dress (I mean rotary torment).

Hey Kids!—Having been interested in reading these cases of "Injuries of the
Head" reported in your Journal by Professor Shipman, of Cortlandville, N.Y.,
I am induced to offer you the notes of a very severe, singular, and, so far as the
result is taken into accounting hitherto unparalleled case, of that class of
injuries, which has recently fallen under my own care....

obvious liar
          Indian fighter
                    candidate for unmarked grave

pismire utterance
          gravel-throated nondescript
                    hat on head
                              & always rain-stained hat

beneath a buttermilk sky
          & sweat rotting shirt pits

                    & a smell that draws flies

but lookit he says
        lookit & he trembles
                the yellowed clip into yr. palm

find the one truth about him
        grins black teeth
                scarred cheek

        stitched socket eye
                jaw knockt out of plumb
                        comic bantering

(amber provokes urine, chatting,
drinking to drive away the time)

but see the heavy eye
        keen, searching for a tool
                to break a box

hands moving among innovative keys coins
        weighing shifting touching the textures

was married he says
        where?
                prepared piano.

& kids?
        Had 'em. See the grin,
                back hand gobbing at the sockets.

Drinking hard?
        Not overmuch
                Where you work last?

Farming help.
        Ever been in jail?
                Nope. (But see the pirana!)

"Hey, fa fa Fuck you silver joe."
all the room's silences included in the performance.

                "A rat creeps in the kitchen"
                "His head a burning house."

The new come man said so.

But let us go a step further. Allow the sun's rays
to fall on a good glass prism and project the
rainbow colors on the nearest wall

WITHOUT ONCE DESCRIBING IT

Tumefaction of the face considerable (1823–1866)
Discharge from the wound & sinus
Restless & delirious
Passed a probe to the base of the cranium without giving pain.
The remainder being ejaculated from the mouth—

GAGE

Exhibit 5.

...we may judge that the body of a living man differs from that of a dead man just as does a watch or other automaton (i.e. a machine that moves of itself), when it is wound up and contains within itself the corpreal principle of those movements for which it is designed along with all that is requisite for its action, from the same watch or other machine when it is broken and when the principle of its movement ceases to act.

Selected Poems

Poetry And Prose

1.

an empty birdcage
of wooden dowels

in a cellar.
the sound of a house   repairs

the lack of song
with the creaking of the stairs.

we carry the cage
to the kitchen, scrub

it white, perform ablutions
upon the prison floor

where so many tough feet
landed in mid-flight

in a slurry of seed,
then hang it on a hook

in the livingroom,   near
the nest of the doorbell

whose double chimes
mechanically replace

gone warbling,
yet the spirit of this place

is not a bird's.
but something more ponderous

tries to climb inside
the door &

cannot fit petitely;
soon it overflows

the cage of song
into featherless prose

that squats compactly
on the arabesques

of the oriental rug
& will not raise its head

higher than
the baseboards

where the barred
shadow

of the empty cage, pins
the yellow wall

exactly where it is.

2.

a roar & a chirrup
wake me

from my sleep:
the potential of a bird

& a chain-mail
beast

face each other
from across

a white expanse;

one flies precisely
its crested head cocked;

the other digs deeply
& licks at the rock.

There

There in that collapsing shed near the pond i waited hearing
my own heart feeling the clutch of the summer heat in my throat
where the dragonflies witched each freshet to its source
where the worm flew on its secret thread i was alone
with the light on the broken floor the mice that crept forth
to leap and tumble on kangaroo legs and all the small things
giving themselves to zero the sparrow with wasps tunneling
her breast the moth with the beetle probing its gilled belly
until it stiffened to a frost-colored stillness.
in one corner a rusted clock rammed with farm grit, chicken feathers,
and the plow tipped on its side like an iron shoe
alive with a dance of spiders. goodbye i said goodbye
the smell of moldy corn cobs—i did not know why i said
goodbye. all the small things shifting in silence as the summer day
darkened, the shadow on the broken floor my antipodes
rushing, rushing to meet me.

To Johns Hopkins University

I pick up my pen
think of my mother sitting cross-legged
smoking a Camel
in her belly a truck-driver's soul
tucks flesh around itself

midnight highway/oiled mirror
fish slap tails on its black surface

pick up my pen
think of Jesus (the fisherman) Blake
exploring the seven wonders of
a shoe factory
his face an oiled mirror/ a

STITCHER! STRIKE BREAKER!

(please)
think of a cloudy anvil
lightning like a scar's reflection
unzips all over
the back seat
suddenly you have eight sides, friend!

think of a man
who wears a cloud
his face an oiled mirror
a piston in a shoe factory
while his mother sits cross-legged
smoking a Camel
a truck driver growing big
between her legs

thinking of asphalt
think of asphalt

pick up my pen
put it down
pick up my pen
put it down
I'm making a shoe, mother!
I'm driving a truck, friend!

I was a carpenter, Magus
son of dirt-farmers, anvil.
these words shipped from shoe factory
to this University
in a carton marked GRAVE DIGGER! HOD CARRIER!

I pick up my pen.
I put down my pen.

To Hart Crane

Stir mud with
a blue claw, Crab,
       watch
the head rise
with a wave, then drop.
       It is
a sea change, a
something rich & strange
gathering sharp kisses
from the beaks of gulls
       who scream
adoration to the
Sun-poet   jaw eroded
by the tides.

Prospero returned
by the obedient waves,
       see the armored children run
aslant across that
meteoric brow.
       Each bone gem-like
in its web of flesh, dismantled neatly
       like a word uncoined;
       he joins
the crush of ciliated angels
resurrected in a drop of foam
       & lives as resonant
       as one fierce line
beached & bleaching on the wooden page.

To Leibnitz From Japan

KNIFE ON THE CUTTING BOARD: rice fields hurtling by train windows:
tombo, or dragonfly, amembo, or water strider, whatever--however--
you call them: at work, alive, skating on shadows, the dim
slither of energies/spiral churning up through earth through sky:
bird hovering midway in air between our eyes and the dun cliff
face sinuous with fog crying an urgent *ree ree ree*: & those on the
street hurrying to shelter from the tin roof rattling typhoon boiling
up from nowhere: where am I in this tangle of obliquities: right here
squarely before you/mirror in my hand now lost beneath your
nostrils is a joke or not: the shed collapses, herons take shelter
in a celery stalk tree, the river the color & consistency of curdled
milk & you the recipient of the moment: happy to be here beyond
the pig's head turning yes & no at rusted chain's end, beyond the dog
jerked upright to an old man's posture. All happy, as I said, (& why not?) to be

where the eye brocades disembarks disembrains
in such manner: 0 & 1, 0 & 1, as it turns.

Alchemical Lion

1.
The lion bounds forward on paws
Wide as lightning, light as laughter,
Leaps from the heavens,
Hurdles us, contains us
In a belly of iron
& Ivory   for a century.
Ultimately humbles us.

Lion whose brain is an elastic sea
See us shivering beneath the
Sky. Be not unfriendly
To us, Cat—
& Roar to the mirroring
Heavens that they contain
You safely

As you held us
Between your lips
In savage definition.

2.
We turn you around
Flesh rains from your bones.
Yellow King, you are laughing;
You consider us
From your hollow sockets
With claws
Permanently extended.

We catch you
In a crystal globe
& Threaten to eat you

As you devoured us
One pulse ago.

You are still laughing
In your flooded cage
Your bones are thirsty
You say.
We pour quick-
Silver   You

Foot a dance
With a peacock's step
Then tumble your Wife
The Lunar Lioness
& Hoarsely purr.

We turn away:
We are your children:
We must stoke the fire
& Approve

       of your hot love.
       the light of your combustion
       'fills the desert

       & a golden hive
       floats above
       your bones.

Still Life With Dragonfly

The void's struck through it & opened dun bells
behind the dried blisters of the eyes & within
the legs a chaos heaved & spread itself in a claw
weakly grappling August light

now laved in September light
made brittle by sun's heat
with dust & husks & cigarette butts upon the sill

prismatic wings
stiffened like paddles
no longer stir the lion-colored air
but abrade away with a breath, sinuous

among mite-shredded leaves
conchoid fractures

a dim slither of energy
alive with a dance of spiders

& past the grit on the window

a stone rolls upright
pushed by an old man.

Hero

& I have seen him fallen in the dust,
head blank as a bird's
his cudgel bird-headed also—
The copter blades of the Bull of Heaven
mixing the colors of the sky
in a dry bowl

                    Have seen him
                    rise on his stick-like legs

phallus like a thorn
& challenge this self-same Bull of Heaven
with nacreous claws
while the stars
like wounded aurochs
pale in the jungle distance
& god is
a severed head
in a helmet of thunder.

For he was born from the Rock—(one eye eternally
            open on the void)—
He carved himself from the Rock
& drove his furrow in the female grain;
stone glittered in his mouth before he spoke

Stone crumbled in his mouth before he wept
inside the skull's parentheses. From his forehead
leaned a granite crown
the size of Jesus in a blaze of sparrows

And all the valveless fury of his flesh
sprang the death's head from its amber prison
bruised the indehiscent into Spring
forced the incoherent into song—

Stone blossomed in his mouth before he sang.

Holderlin's Cabinet

Dear Friends
it is not enough to develop
a vocabulary sufficient to express
light in a dark mirror
    Owl
      in horned
        moon   gravity
or riot & growing displeasure
the fork-tailed utterance

    sun
deboned above the sea   dollops
of shit that harden into coins

Friend w/the face
of Eagle Lion Man
tautologies explode above the midden heaps
it is not enough
to tell you what you mean to me direct
    communication
    w/the
    Dead

bread crumbs burst into roses
tin leaves brighten w/blood
    meat hooks orbit w/the weight
      of the confirmation
      of tragedy beyond
      silence

Take away breath, Friend,
    & lips collapse upon
      themselves
      the song   leaches
      into cooling furnace sand &

becomes a bas-relief
chariot race   or a tiger
gored by an Etruscan bull

To a Bird Killed on a Power Line

Little balancer
(Phlebitic knot in the leg
Of a dancer)
Watch me watching
You walk
To the black
Pole
Where one claw
Grounds you
Breaks your wings
With a lightningbolt:
Muffled pop
Magnetic blood
Frothes your beak. Gray
Feathers gap
The directions
While you are plugged in
No more bird
But an electrode
Singing megawatts. Un-
Houseled metaphysical fire,
Frying & falling
Cleaner than you were:
Lice cooked at your eye
In mid suck,
A song still boils
In your throat.

He Brings the Honey to Us Without Fear

a.
Gravity is the ghost in the stone & it is far cleaner
than blood, or even magnetism with its burred tongue of iron
giving the lie to space. What you glimpse from
your eye's corner may be the counterweight of a distant
star, or the letter A thrown down on its side
in the murk of heaven.

b.
bow kills
& lions, what do they know?
only
"bow kills"
& "lions, what do they know?"
To cure a wound
in the hand
write
"in the hand"
on your hand
& lick it off.

c.
& what about this man whose face
disappears behind a mask of golden bees
beating wings in unison? Is he stung
in an ochre cloud of shame? No, he
brings the honey to us without fear.

Lexical Obelisk

where have we been
to lose so much. where
in the dark world did
we stand and for how
long. while magpies
cried above our heads and
shadows hobbled our
feet. while the locked
nostrils opened like death
and lean men dowsed
our pockets for loose change.
what did we do to help the rocks
grow in their secret chambers
underground?

nothing. says the father. it's
important to lift and carry
whatever is before us. a sentence
or a keg of nails. without quailing.
without asking for a drink.
without naming or dividing or
hitch hiking or sitting down. in a
strange place never ask directions, but
know the number of perishable goods
nor waste time blubbering over a secret task.
ask the mirror and it will hand you
nails. ask a hammer and it will whisper
its own steel logic. carry this thorn in
your ear and it will inspire you
to have children: a boy and a girl.
teach them to work eternally.
teach them to forget themselves
and become an object in the errant matrix
of the world.

the father knows you. you hear him
in a dark room working mother's assembly
line. pulling something apart.
putting something together. he might
use language then. divide! is his command
and you must answer with a saw's precision.

father moves on metal rails
in mother's body. he is a hard worker.
his hands know the grain of
the sky. run a splinter of blue
under his thumbnail: he bleeds khaki.

I raise a sentence in your honor:
lexical obelisk, black, truncated,
lightning bolt aground, older than
fire, earth, flood. every clattering

tongue is leashed there: Papa,
father of silence, thick
groaning thunderer before the
midnight televisions of memory, here is

a statement worthy of you. a
reply from a cowardly son too fond
of ease. who could not hammer.
who could not run the machines.

Paper Devil

1.

The paper devil came on stilts
To see me. He was a wicker man
More pagan than Christian
And he winked into my highest window.
I laid my pen aside
And cried 'No More, I Will Abroad!'
Struck the metaphysical sails of my conceit
And turned on the Television.

When I'd finished battering my brain
With nerveless images more numerous than squid
Laid in a pile of moldering luminescence
Upon the shores of an outlandish sea,
I hid my stinging eyes behind two hands
Clapped together around a bit of air
And did the grand ventriloquist act of prayer
Answering myself in a true basso profundo.

2.

The devil remains unconvinced.

3.

Grown weary of the weight
Of iron-bound words in hasps of gold, my jaw
Hangs like a broken branch and moves
Willy-nilly with the winter wind. My tongue

Finds its ruptured cage congenial
And sounds the dark sky with its fork;
While the paper devil warms to his work,
Bends his drizzling beard above my shadow
And licks the stain from the inkpot Luther threw.

4.

I shrive him with a matchbox reliquary:
A saint's head black with visions arcs
Kingdoms of cold oblivion
Where random signals splay into the void.
There he follows the stations of the cross
Knee-deep in ashy mummers, a rosary of fuses in his hand;

Adjusts his crown with a garish claw
And cacks delight at entropy's alchemy
As it turns cathedrals into golden rubble, Petrarchan
Tape loops into celluloid fossils; then drags me by an elbow

To a window where I see
The spontaneous combustion of men everywhere.

Imitation of Keats

I don't picture my reflection in the
mirror of Art/ is Art a mirror?
& The reflection doesn't wish to
think; but it's hungry,
& it's afraid/it suffers/it's
sad/—everything they say you
shouldn't say too loud up here
on Parnassus without spearing
your cheek with the nearest forked tongue,
raking space with smart
quotation marks. It's
too late for your basic legend of Keats:
I've outlived him anyway & fucked too much for
that scene: coughing blood
once or twice into the old top hat
& kicking off. (I like girls too much to die!)
But really—yawn once. Take this honest hand.
Here leans one whose name is writ

as writ.

Jesse

no good dreams like the other night
just screaming
into a black mirror;
in that dream
I'd returned to an old love   a Chicago painter
who bled me blind   my fist slams into
                                       plaster walls
                                       I bray like the ass I was

                  feeling the old
antipathies

return   Rub my eyes
because I'm finally awake & how do
you do/ to make me calm? How do
you do (?)   You're with me again
across the table addressing

a postcard to your Wolfie Otto
          6230 Frankfurt 80.
Coffee cup dear we're all slowly dying but
you trimmed my beard this morning
can reach all the hard places. Remember?
          I made you cum. Don't
blush at that line. Now I finally

recall lying drunk all one fine summer's day
                        in the long grass.
A dog sniffed my face. 2 kids
came round to say hi. The sky
was a dime store window trimmed with white & blue clouds.

I was ready to burglarize heaven any minute
                 for fun
make all the alarms ring
without a thought of consequences

    (because I'm ardent)
steal all the angels' panties
            (because I'm still alive)
wear them like a cock's comb, red-
lace-heart-first
on my head
& crow liberty! fraternity! equality!

over a wall of fog
to you mine "Germ Girl," O
best & happiest
lover   please

keep the 2 syllables
of my name.

New Years Day

blinds up
the whole story wobbles by
like the steam-driven panoramas painted by the eccentric
South Dakotan artist John Banvard:
"A TRIP DOWN THE MISSISSIPPI."
"A HISTORY OF THE WORLD FROM THE TIME OF NOAH."
"THE TRUE IDENTITY OF THE INDIANS AS THE LOST TRIBES OF
        [THE HEBREWS."

the story bangs along for two hours,
unrolled from
log-sized cylinders, and
for my 25 cents
I can see Anthony & Cleopatra in a peeling embrace,
the building of the Great Wall of China,
a panorama of the Midwestern holy lands blessed by a Mormon Jesus.

—Now—

a new roll turns on its spindle
here comes 1984...
As I see it from 807 E. Juneau,
city of Milwaukee, Milwaukee County,
the state of the world
is in fairly good shape,
the birds are in working order
(a raven squats on a frozen limb even as I speak)
none of the cathedrals that line this street
have tiptoed away during the night, so
they must yet serve some function,
people still drink milk in their morning coffee,
therefore cows exist,
and gravity works
(bread crumbs
drop to the roaches)

& yes
people still get
hang-overs
from too much Jack Daniels the night before

—turn, turn—

A lady I once kept at lips' length
is now one hemisphere and six hours' difference
from this time zone gone,
obviously memory is still here when I need it
love needs no new fuses
and hate in its little black box
hums merrily on.
A new being
waits in a hidden sack
for the green light
and his Mama's go-ahead
to call me Daddy.
I wait for this year
to ease up out of the muck
like a monster pig
chewing a colossal sugar beet
to sweeten its breath.
So I can finish this panorama
the pig must be trained
to stand on a gilded pedestal
and grunt dixie.
But I have plenty of time to marshal the minutes—
the boilers hiss with a good head of steam. I lean
        on the starlit throttle...
the cylinders groan,
the frayed canvas unrolls,
and off we go lurching
into my thirtieth year.

Nagasaki

Where the Dutch savants

rolled forth Paracelsus

> like a cast-iron golem
> (a doll pulled upright by a team of oxen)
> fed to the translators

Newton's *Principia, De Rerum Natura*
> as lion heads to starlings
> parrot tongues to sea bream
> fingers slit for sucking cuckoos

> grape louse, ebiont, decanting
> redacting, cheating, teaching, translating

> fearful tales
> out of purgatory

> earthquakes in Macau
> examples of false miracles

> psalterize, enigmatize
> spoon away the richest peacock blood
> lips luminous with fat

> young men weep like wax
> beneath the bailiff's sword

> unlearning the fateful numbers of Descartes
> beside the decimal river

caged icons risible for half-an-hour
> squalid parades in the rain
> gouged in boards

by practiced burins

long-nosed foreign women
unlaced their secrets
for the tonsured artists
ink in every gland

& the doctors had to dance & box
    feign fright on command
    add, subtract, act monkey-like
    sheep-like (& bedlamite)

cavort upon straw mats
    strike copper bells & sing

    hey ding-a-ding!

& fell in love with blushless
    inamoratas   kimono-clad
    gigglers taught the Gnostic
    way to pleasure
    so no blood would mix or spill

then died of pox
typhus
cholera

or lived to turn it all to **Text**.

The Altered Voice

Incorporate an environment into the poem
take breath from somewhere
put it here. Can you tell
if I'm male or female. Don't
panic. Cover my name
with flour or volcanic ash
cover my name with mud
mustard seed or powdered beryllium. But
American poetry of note is meant to be language
at its most memorable as in Ms. C.S.

writing about her baby or
Ms. E.S. writing about the joys
of her baby so I shall write about
a stone baby cut free from ambiguities
by continual hammer blows delivered to the
chisel lisping numbers steel-toothed

shrieking or singing its way into atom-clotted
lattices debitage falling dust spiraling heat
rolling up into the calamitous sky, each metallic bite
registered in the sculptor's canines, nasal cavities, sinuses, upper
chest. Each stroke prizing apart, levering, pulverizing
leveling   am I male or female yet can this be
crippled into politics haven't I seen you

elbowing into a room
repeated indefinitely, cluttered with tropes
randomly wandering, dazed nude stuttering
among the trophies of our mnemonic museum
(smell of furrowed brows, forced confessions, cocktails among the
chips & spalls.) I set the stone baby on end by a lake
of half-remembered sunsets so at sunrise
people can choose one memorable detail (perhaps
a hieroglyph) to stack away bound in yellowing covers
thus a legend is born or is that a wanton myth

I set the stone baby on end by a lake
of vaguely-remembered sunsets so at dawn
mysterious masses can decide on one
shared experience to be recounted, but the curves
of the stone baby will cast an articulate shadow eclipsing
the wrist of anyone who dares to set the granite enfant
on end by a lake of half-remembered sunsets
so at sunrise whole populations can choose this memorable detail
to bind and stack away in yellowing covers. Perhaps this is a myth. Complexity
builds as the breath from one side of a thought experiment
is allowed by a Scottish demon to slink mere molecules at a time
to the other, less spirited, side. I must decide if I am
a man or a wanton woman as I move, three steps forward,
clap hands, then two steps back, across the noumenal ground of the poem
the phenomenal baby in the crook of an arm remaining constantly
itself, even as I shift even as I turn, or stop
to set it down before the giggling savants
who continue to pull at my veil. I step into the coolness
of the mnemonic museum, sit before the bust of my
granite enfant, a nation suffering in my arms. It is
sunrise and the one memorable detail you will choose is not my name.

On Handel's Suite For Harpsichord No. 5 In E Major

Ants explore a cowrie shell
on the windowsill

while Handel's Harmonious Blacksmith
underscores the cog-like movements

of the light as it falls
through broken leaves crushing green

maps of Hyperborea & the ogham of leaf veins
against the glass.

One ant lifts mandibles against a rush of air
breaks salt sea-rust from the wall

of the pink inner lip, then lifts the cube
like an ensign and tractors backwards

down ledge into the familiar track
of its own scent woven outwards

by hidden glands to disappear
within a churning tumulus of monads
held within a grid of genetic directives.

There, within that order, the Queen performs
her ancient function: minting oblong tokens

of life in death—those honey-embalmed exoskeletons
that will carve their way to life

and immediately understand
the lineaments of a need larger than their own
craving for sugared moisture—

mandibles ready to clutch and carry,
lift, tug, swivel, roll out instant order

as staves direct these tiny shocks of music
along their rungs

to march in the formal garden of the ear
and spread their sonic burdens on the air,

climbing within these brittle, harpsichorded spirals,
then probing silence like a shell's dry curve

until it folds itself in summer
and applause.

Lecturing on Walt Whitman and Emily Dickinson in China

I celebrate myself
And what I assume you shall assume,
For every atom belonging to me as good belongs to you...
There is no heat here.
The girl in front has ring worm of the scalp,
the shy man sitting by himself has fever-clouded eyes & a consumptive's
          cough,
but they are smiling. The Indonesian
beauty with one small black spot on her perfect
front tooth huddles with the others in the damp. Some
scrub Reeboks over the gritty floor
as I explain Walt's intricacies, stage his barbaric yawp. They ask
politely, why is Miss Dickinson
so concerned with heaven? A few have bound
their copies into books
with kittens and blue birds on the covers.

Beyond the bars on the windows
one sees a boundless falling away
of palm trees broken bottles used kotex plastic and weeds
under a sky fat with the burgeoning rainy season.
Mosquitoes whiz and hurtle through the air. From the distance floats
klaxons of trucks, busses and cars cacophonious
near lunch hour as they barrel to Quinzhau,
narrowly missing walkers in straw hats, bicyclists,
pull motors lurching on the shoulders of the roads;
all things Chinese super-freighted with granite, cloth, wood, bricks
          and babies.
And above us, everywhere, speakers
rust on poles like low-tech idols. Cords snake & flap. I smile,
look into every eye as I explain
the uncertainties of life in 19th-century America
how the infinite could arrive in a virus, then unfold oppressive galaxies
where the only sound permitted was the buzzing of a fly, but a sudden
          bell

devours my voice
and all stand at once. Then
the speakers replace our private thoughts
with words large & tawdry as the billboards in the muddy fields.

On Soutine's "Carcass of Beef"

it hangs
   in space illusory
as a dream of deserts
   in a dark room

alive with the motor thrum of flies

   we get a long lingering look
at its iridescent gut
   like a cheesecake shot
   from an old Life backpage

   legs spread shamelessly

   the drip drip drip
   of that dark blood
   congealing on the cement

Soutine, the flesh of your hands
has fallen from fierce bone

thick, sensuous lips have given way
to bleached teeth clamped on deutsch marks

all the chickens you captured   wrung necks
& plucked
before you framed their immortality
give thanks to a convulsive god

all the fish on sawdust-covered tables
stare back through sockets larded with vermilion

as you stab the canvas
with a cheap stilleto
& rip it across the grain
toward you—Soutine
terror of collectors

it's not cold enough
to keep beef
still   see?
it writhes on its hook,
a worm on an iron thread

it weeps its truth like a wounded zealot

we must turn away
or asperge ourselves with smoke
from the butcher house, & like Soutine

clasp the smokestacks familiarly

yell the empty song
in airless rooms

kiss the reflection
in the pool of blood.

The Blues

I hold my face in my hands & give
My sorrows to those brilliant moaners:
Blind Lemon, Tommy Johnson, Robert Johnson

& Yes, I shake my head yes, remembering
An empty bed, a gap-toothed smile,
A train rolling from the platform,
The suitcase in my hand, searching for my gal.

I grow conked hair, a tongue thick as hootch-assisted sorrow,
Am walking to Chicago to dine on sawdust
& drink canned heat in a one-room shack waiting for Jesus
To deal out judgement like a deck of cards.

I'm down on my knees, Lord,
Looking up the store-bought skirt
Of Bessie Death, the poison, Lord,
Sanctifying my brief & furious life.
I'll go outside & sleep face-down in a snowdrift

My guitar in a pawnshop on 21st & Fayette,
Furious husbands pounding on the door,
Frantic to pluck the secret of my gift
From a black mouth caged but not imprisoned by six strings.

Bluesmen tell me
"Good woman's hard to find."
Their spirit voices crackling
From the speaker. Imprisoned

In the body's needs long after
The body falls away-
They leave behind a residue, a smoky yowl,
A dull knife weaving through space:
Mallarme's *parole essentielle*, perhaps,
Or only a "Yaz Yaz Yaz."

In The Cold

1.

I was thinking how the lake
drags under a bit of the city

with each wild grab
like a desperate man in a crowded bar

reaching for the till
before he runs.

2.

I was thinking of the snow flakes
cut by the drop-hammers of the sky

& how the ice never melts
on the angels in the Polish cemetery

where the dead lie
rib to rib in the cold.

3.

I was thinking of all coverings
abruptly ripped away

of the brain's heat tumbling
up & up--lost in a copper cloud

of a warm breath
squandered on a mirror

& of dull eyes staring at black water.

4.

I was thinking of a weeping picture
of the mother of god

& how, at night,
in the dim cathedral

the heat clicks on

to keep the miracle warm.

5.

I was thinking of a room
so empty--dust echoes.

of a hand wrenched open
like a broken flower

of the brooding stain the woman wears
as she sings to no one on the library steps

& of a rat-toothed wind that can set a dollar bill
soaring
above the ice.

Against The Agony of Matter

1.

Your spine—a fossil flower stem—shifts:
you turn on your side in sleep.

2.

Light shimmers on your brows,
engrailed shields of light

3.

& the dropping away to darkness around each soft eye pit,
the charcoal smudge on rich rag vellum flesh
draws me near to observe your face

4.

relaxed, softly unhinged, uncannily direct—
as bird song beyond midnight is direct—

5.

Behind it that clinch of bone
that could make an old man melancholy
loves me too, I know, presses close so that I

6.

suck my teeth in concern,
for welts rise upon bone & stone & mineral integument,

7.

the starry flail falls without warning
upon us. Ships are known to founder in the tented seas
whose maelstroms

8.

churn away the even shoulders of our island
with every wave unrolling feathered thunder

9.

& the moon siphons forth crystalline fire
from the underpinnings of our rest. Cruel, cruel. Even your hair
feels like toothed rain.

10.

You do not move, but remain Euclidean in repose, safe though
meteors strike the outer layers of our atmosphere and take fire,
tumbling end over end at us, slowly at first, then as dreams

11.

blazing towards utterance & so justify the tongue's vague arching
beneath the palate as I see one flash across the void in this rented room

12.

& attempt to describe it to you in a whisper
you cannot help but ignore. You escape the Agony of Matter
like a leaf in a block of salt,

13.

your repose is of one dreaming of deep water, though all you see
within the domes of your half-closed lids will remain

14.

beyond the descriptive powers of a sleep-torn mouth at dawn.
I open the palmate structure of my bones like a music box

15.

so the dancing beads of blood move tenderly in their circuits, and await
the deconstruction of the hour, for you are my meditation upon a blank wall,

16.

my fuming away of every eventuality
& lovely death of machines. Never kiss me. Never open your eyes.

Swedenborg's Airplane: A Hymn (1745)

To be sung in the subjunctive mode...

He bobbled like a toy
        upon unanswered prayers. He worked
                his crimson oars as whales
                        move their sluggish fins; his blank face
                                was a wooden bead & brain hermetically sealed
                                englobed his gifted creed.

We did not see him sweat
        or look upon the ground.
                The rumble of Vesuvius
                        did not adjust his eye.

We lauded his invention
        threading the autumn breeze:
                a triumph allowed to man just once
                        by the love of a God who lathed
                                the bumble bee from Perfect Mind
                                      & set it among the forms
                                            subject to poverty.

The jesus-colored wings
        lightly scissored sky,
                the rudder like a sparrow's tail
                        preserved him in the deeps beyond
                                rude fumblings of our science.

We drew his toil with our pens.
                (Distance made him doll.)
                      Madness made him brave
                              to swag above the towers;
                              he saw no angels there.

                                        We did not see him fall.

                                        We did not see him fall.

Hallucigenia

I walk on compass points through hell
tip lymph-engorged gristle
of my ill-favored trunk & tripod forward while

seven back-hinged pincers snap bacteria from murk
& funnel edible crumbs into an ever-busy gullet
digesting motile star dust and the chaff of atoms.

I wring my anus upward & release
green floats that cloud the silver verso-waves
of Pre-Cambrian shallows
topped with sulfuric flares
no pseudo-lung dare guzzle

& inch the measures of despair
across the not-yet-ancient sands:
(my gait the demiurgic law
parsing out topologies of noughts).

Brainless, eyeless,
yet with the curve of beauty
in an empty cheek

I move as randominity decrees
my own unheeded oracle,
die & become a freak
shimmer of life in stone.

A MAN STANDS IN THE YELLOW AIR IN A FIERY GLOBE OF MY HEIGHT, ACCOMPANIED WITH SOME HUNDRED OF PUPPETS, ONE OF WHICH SAYS:

"malkuthic blood
"finds
"habitation in any
"altitude, astounding
"the precise observer
"w/ ebullient
"displacements, how it
"pushes as Vasco da Gama
"pushed for the edge
"of the world, from which
"it promptly falls & pools
"beyond the tapir-sniff
"of polite conversation, where
"it establishes its
"brown pagoda, weathering
"the hours, stiffening
"to artifact, comet trail,
"pigment w/out canvas.

"flowers forth,
"geysers up,
"leans a ruby staff
"breaks it
"against a wall
"lies low & hunkers,
"a lizard sluggish
"in the palm. The flash
"of the razor blade wheeling
"over,
"a silver bird
"clacking its beak
"in triumph. The flash
"of the fat bullet

"buzzing the raw flowers
"black,
"a touch of vermillion in each trumpet—

Agla Agla
Elohim, Zevoath

"Lame foot reshaped becomes
"a piston in a trivial machine
"hands
          "glowing nubs
"spine
          "steel pipe
"skin
          "a net of golden links
"cut clean
          "of human minutes

Agla Agla
Elohim, Zevoath

now wounded space comes to cover you like a man:
each wire bites flesh with linear jaw
reticulations pack the sky
w/a clatter of dry sockets. Lie beneath these many nothings
let them gride against your skin like miller's grit
your lover's voice a wasp in an inverted bowl
scratching a sting against dull matter

wires thread veins,
knot in silver coils behind each eye
winched by chain
sway on flayed heels sins/ sluice away
through cut wrists pierced heart slit lungs
wasps push jaws of grit across each empty dial of bone
your arid music strung from earth to sky,

gravity wobbling the rockets
you sing within the furnace
dear face
muted by jade tiles   Great Face calling
cell on cell on cell of Malkuth
haunted zeroes rimmed by cusps of ice

the wind lends you eloquence of empty jars in storm
to answer up the mighty stations of the breath

hand me your deafness, hand me
the hole in your lung, hand me the stitch
in the palm of your hand, the stone beneath your tongue
with the red thread through it
double the hymning lattices, the overlapping
dimensions, a crown of wood
a crown of iron with copper fasteners
a crown of terra cotta

come seal the seven openings of the body
with plugs of jade
& lapis lazuli, a polished disc pierced through at the top of the head
left open to admit one whispered sutra
a drop of mercury crimped inside each node

a labyrinth rolls back before the breath
solid breath, broken breath
caged in hexagrams
set like apiaries in the snow
we dance as we mourn

with eyes soulful as rotten wheat
we exult   crush metal shards against the emptiness
the cold wind cannot pierce metal casings
bitten breath cannot bleed

This Word

This word
begets itself
as in: stallion's hooves/mare's back
      the alembic surfeited, stretched
            watched w/out embarrassment
in a field hock deep in reddest mud

or as the inverted tan triangles
marching on the iridescent lip of the cowrie
vitrify to a bronze & cream tattoo

one complex, self-regulating system finds another until a room, a stanza,
          a prison is built

& we lie hidden
beneath the straw
recalling the elegant question
at the edge
of waking:
WHAT DO WE DESIRE?

escape from the boundaries
  (of distance)
   (of body)
     the forest of moral cacti
      & beyond that the
         infinite field of
           black rubble
        unrolled in sunleached
           murals
      on bullet-riddled walls

WHAT DO WE DESIRE?

escape from the limitations

of pocketbook
   intellect
     Yes & No
thin loops of paradigmatic structures
        enameling clay

those limitations
that force us underground
in the long low houses
of silence
    when we should be
    walking upright
    brainpans
    shattering
    the skies.

WHAT DO WE DESIRE?

only a burning wheel
rolled down-hill
thru industrial valleys
only the words "proleptic voice"
chalked on a culvert
by anonymous hands
only the crooked street
at dawn

     (the letter Q
breaching virtual space
to proclaim itself god--
What god?)

WHAT DO WE DESIRE?

to throw ourselves free
from the tops of steeples?

turn stones
to speckled bread?
own & command
the ordinary city?

(& rise in a sunburst
as in some Persian
miniature
in which the
scimitar falls
& the blood explodes
from the heart!)

If words were first pellets of clay

ALIEN HAND,
then take these words &
break them down
into those magic pellets again.
    mark an X for
the lovers who stare at all-night streets
put the X right here,
        ALIEN HAND.

say, one: THE SKY
    two: THE MINERAL SOCKETS OF THE SEA
      & three: A FALSE, ENTROPIC BEAUTY
          SCOURED AWAY BY LICHEN & METEORITE
          PULVERIZED BY A BREATH
          say it

        Because you can

        X & X &—O!—

Then drop these pellets of clay
    ALIEN HAND
into a copper cup & on them pour some wine

    Red or White

Whatever vintage you may choose

& quaff it off

    as the old poets wrote

    Or knock it back

However you may choose

To term the process

ALIEN HAND

Context a Babylonian froth beached upon the upper lip

& grit between the teeth & in the gizzard
To signify a signalizing breath

Then sing:

"I am freeing a flake of beauty
"From nothingness now, something as permanent
"As the shoe found 3 yards deep beneath a battlefield
"& in it, tender bones!"

Sing this song because the Muses are out there

Someplace

ALIEN HAND

Blowing their spit-filled whistles in the cold.

Mayakovsky Is Dead

Where's the joint of Nita Joe?
Nita's joint is just below!

Mayakovsky knew
that bullets turn to poetry
in Bagdadi Russia between dusk and dawn.
He thought perhaps in Moscow it was the same.
He also knew to get ahead
he had to catch the fame train early.

BUT

first he wondered where to aim his Poetry Gun—
down his throat maybe?
Should he suck the bullet out?
Draw on it like a clit?
Should he wrap his tongue around the barrel thinking
Lenin? Stalin? Choke the death seed down hoping
that it breaks the spine w/ an incredibly sweet snap?
Should he perhaps aim it at his brow
ready to begin the revolution at the count of three?

1,2...

Mayakovsky wished his gun were bigger
for his pistol shrank each time he pulled the trigger.

Should a man write odes about Ford trucks? Ask
Mayakovsky who says:
"Forget your 'Wooden Russia' w/ candles scorching the Virgin's double chin!
We have new cars to race, new enemies to wrestle!
The celestial timer is ticking, Citizens! Here is the hammer and here is the steel.
Strike quickly and a rocket will rise like a prayer
to shatter on tomorrow's perfect streets!"

Point your Poetry Gun in the air:
    bang! bang! bang! Comrade.
The moon steams on its rails over the Urals.
I love you like a one-legged soldier
loves his leg, Babushka.

    Wicked Paris woman waiting on the bed,
would you care to conceive good Russian sons?

                             NO!

    Aim your gun Mayakovsky:

BANG:

      Gobble your pineapple,
      Chew at your grouse,
      Your last day is coming, you bourgeoisie louse.

We celebrate radios, aeroplanes, hammer on iron,
iron bent in the shape of a woman, Cubist paintings,
Charleston, Fox Trot, Negro jazz.
Why?...Because!...Exactly!...Citizens, listen
to this important announcement:
      Hard-hearted Hannah
      The Vamp of Savannah
      The Vamp of Savannah
      Gee-ay.

Workers forward! Factories in place of museums!
The tire recapper's sweating dance is more beautiful
    than the arabesques of 1000 Nijinskies!

Mayakovsky points his gun
    at the lion-colored clouds.

Points his silver-triggered gun
                              at mother tundra, father taiga.
Aims his six-shooter under the table,
                              "Let's see them cards!"
he yells at Carl Sandburg. Marinetti
                              marvels
at Mayakovsky's markmanship:
                              how magnificent
manifestations of tomorrow manifest themselves in myriads
from Mayakovsky's magnetic manipulations.

        Q. Why did Mayakovsky cross Red Square?
           A. To get to the other side.
        Q. What's Blok and white and red all over?
           A. Mayakovsky.

        //

    O you shootnik, shoot it out!
    O you shootnik, shoot it forth!

You who shoot both up and down
Shoot along so shootingly
    Shoot it off dynamically.
Shooter of the shooting shootniks, overshoot the shootathons!
Aimer of Poetic Pistols, countershoot the Kingdom's shots!
    Bangio! Crackio!
    Discharge, recharge, chargelets, banglets,
Aim your Pistol high and low.

    O you shootnik, shoot it out!
    O you shootnik, shoot it forth!

        //

Mayakovsky admires himself even now.

107

Mayakovsky was Billy the Kid in another incarnation.
Mayakovsky eternally wins the race.

Mayakovsky signs and countersigns.
Mayakovsky is not jealous of Gorky, or Pasternak; neither
is he awed by Tolstoi. He handles official matters
with the deft touch of any Rimsky-Korsakov.

"Hand me another, and quickly!" roars Mayakovsky.
Mayakovsky met Sophocles in Hell the other night. They
dropped their eyes and advanced w/ clenched fists. We
were waiting for a confrontation. The air was electrified
w/ suppressed emotion. Sophocles spat in Mayakovsky's face...
This was the first and only time we've seen Mayakovsky back down from a fight.

//

His **HEART** was a 50,000 pound boiler ready to rupture.

His **GUN** was a wolf w/ circular teeth.

His **HEART** was a smiling athlete strolling along a sandy beach.

His **GUN** was a pimply man w/ nowhere to go.

His **HEART** was a unicycle the size of an explosion.

His **GUN** was built of interlocking contradictions.

His **HEART** screamed down at his groin: "Get me some air!"

His **GUN** grew split hooves and chased magpies in the thickets.

His **HEART** was a long-fingered woman w/ her hair tied in knots.

His **GUN** pounded its fist and wanted to know the reason why.

BULLET

like a young hound tasting blood
for the first time.

You rest now in a scarlet castle awaiting the Master's key.
What poems did Mayakovsky think of then? Did he, like Esenin, have the sense
to write them down? And how many factories gave mandatory overtime
ON THAT WONDERFUL DAY?

MELVILLE BEAT WIFE FOR BOTCHED BOOK!

& how can we read it without thinking of Mrs. Melville?

Euripides speaks of some
'marriage songs of shepherds'
                    pipe-music
which throws mares
                    into amorous frenzy
& horses mad w/desire
                    to couple.

& the pipe music provides
a marriage song

                    as poetry
the wedding march for Mind and Matter

a blaze of opposites
bone pressed to bone
            lifts
the dynamic structure
            to the sky
                    & Furthermore,

MELVILLE BEAT WIFE FOR BOTCHED BOOK!
say it in conference
                    book store
                            class room
supermarket check-out line
the horrible secret
            daughter Francis hated
            all poetry because of him
                    cld. nt. read Longfellow
                            Whittier, Whitman

or Emily Dickinson

In addition

Rosinius says that he was shown a vision of a man who was dead, & whose body was completely white like salt. His limbs were cut off, & his head was of fine gold but sundered from the body. By him stood a monstrous bald man, ghastly of aspect, a two-edged sword in his hand stained with blood. In his left hand he held a piece of paper on which was written: I HAVE SLAIN YOU THAT YOU MIGHT POSSESS ABUNDANT LIFE: BUT YOUR HEAD I WILL CONCEAL, THAT THE WORLD SHALL NOT SEE YOU. I WILL LAY WASTE YOUR BODY THAT IT MAY BECOME PUTRID AND MULTIPLY ITSELF, & BRING FORTH FRUITS UNNUMBERED—

aborted Pips
conceived between 2
steamboat accidents
twisted poppets
on some ridiculous mission   should these

be shattered on the emerald table
like barbarous charms cut from ivory, then
struck with willow wands
in conference hall
  class room
    text book

This intelligence
draws inward like a sap & rides
the brain's combs like the bitterest honey
& NOW I'M A STUPID POET
(a mirror w/an ear)

staring in amazement at my own hands lifting & letting fall my own hands
counting the scars on my hands

arranging objects in the room not especially to my liking
but **TO THE SUN'S LIKING
& TO THE MOON'S!**

                    & so I rearrange yr. limbs
                          you dead bastard

                              ticked together
                              tocked apart
                    A gigantic doll
                    pulled upright by a team of oxen
                    so its brow trembles
                    above the clouds.

FLASH!

          as of this date No News from Eternity
              where Mrs. Melville sleeps
              in winding sheet & shadow
          her bruises agitated dust, faintly radioactive

                    Draw the cloth away
                          historian
                    jaw drops
                          mouth gapes
                          O'd   in
                    indifference
                    or horror

          AS YOU LOOK AT IT

AS A STONE LOOKS AT IT
as the sea

          Let the doll fall
          at the dictates of the weak force

        cur at its heels
        abyss at its
        toe tips

    & death should be
mutely glorious: a kissing
of concave mirrors
            lapping of black water
                        & the page curls,
                                yellows, softens in the rain.

but say it once more & NEVER FORGET

MELVILLE BEAT WIFE FOR BOTCHED BOOK!
he was obviously a monster.
I wouldn't want him to marry my daughter.

They

Feet nailed
To the dance floor

Their hands arabesqued
Until the attendant
Novocained their hands.

They thrashed heads
While the band howled
But latched neck braces
Made nodding difficult.

Their eyes–their eyes!
Rolled whites rhythmically
Till blindfolded–rhythmless.

Stiffened bodies swayed
But ear-plugs stopped the show
To whispering applause.

Now nailed in upright cases, they
Dance grimly in Effect and Cause.

Legion

hey i recall the last time we made the scene
pulls on her panties, fish nets, adjusts the
(she doesn't need the) bra, buttons blouse over
elegance, rolls sleeves over tracks,
chopsticks in her coiled up hair.
we hustle through march wind. down dismal
streets & I'm careful to hold her up over clustered
ice: doc martens grant more traction than spike
heels. climb the hill cars idling down through
snow blow blue cold. then there's the Torch
& down cellar steps. bubba the bouncer (why
they all named bubba?) sez hello. we're in
free. smiles thaw into scowls because this
is mohawk city and again music and again
meat throb delicious underbump of projectile
sound striking gristle. smoke man. shaved heads
bobbing. fingers punching leather chests/museums
of medals, badges, dangling skulls. suck into
beers. eyes bulge in animated talk or fold away into
heavily-mascaraed sockets like bats into stovepipes.
someone absent-mindedly picks at a scab on a lip,
yet another lifts and lets fall a jangle of
tin-colored fingernails in explanation of some
moot point of neo-fascism. then

THE BOGOMILS mash raw sound into
cement. they got this
old boiler called THE GOD MACHINE
miked up & reverb makes it shake
like a rocket thing in a 50s drive-in movie.
they let it hum and blast our eardrums fuzzy, soon
ZO, the lead screamer, crawls inside and
throws steel dynamic moan:
WAAAAAAAAAAAHHHHHHHHHHHHUUUUUUUUMMMMMMM!
　　　[there's

chico lamort and lisa whirling to the speed guitars,
feeling their leather for a zillion invisible lice, dropping
jackboots among the thousand crushables. high on everything
chico whines spasms claws his face till it
bleeds. like a monk in gasoline flames he's
spazzing in apocalypsis, never saw him look
so good before. & lisa lobbing her prehensile head
to the 4 directions, is pretty as a handgrenade, active as a
bouncing betty. now legion's smiling
o she's taken my hand. & we are up, shoulder to shoulder
thrashing to the wall of sound the fat man with the guitar
& nimble fingers is shoveling our way. our ears are coated
with burning enamel by ZO's suck & squaw
blinded (by his own choice, i hear) by blow torch
to give his moans more soul, & rolling his lidless
eyes as he wails his never-to-be-unnerstood-but-
deep-dude-deeper-than-hell-lyrics through the cheap
p.a. we scream we shout. our throats swell into
leather purses in which our tongues skitter like rats.
chico lamort kicks the wall leaving boot printed
eyesockets of the mohawked skull wall mural
signed 'deadman 8/89.' chico spins like he's outta
his fucking tree but his chick's thrashing to it, & nobody
looks concerned. the Bogomils are smoking into IT.
IT's like blue concentric circles breaking through eyelids
like rank buds of springtime in a cemetery where nobody goes.
our ears are moving along the same high-frequency grid,
now ZO is sweat-wet & naked & yodeling
elvis in hell, & he's not moving a muscle while everybody's
gotta thrash & skank. and legion's face, like it's
dead, but beautiful. and she's got the look of somebody
i once saw knocked down with a shovel by a tripping
freak. stunned-like. but that's beautiful too. it's like
she's got a cum look. like she's getting it and loves it,
and has heaved and moaned at least one time. and look,
this is beyond all suck-ass time. this is the blessed damozel,
the pre-raphaelite wet dream.   see now i know

116

                & now i unnerstand.
                          & i moan it, man
& i wail & hail this girl-star risen high above a fucking factory town
in the miserable midwest. beaming down her black light
so we're all glowing like jimi hendrix on an old poster in somebody's
attic. i can feel it now: she's making us GLOW. don't know if i should
        SHOUT*SHOUT*SHOUT* or sit real quiet like THE THINKER
& sing it low
        then high with falsetto throb & reverb like walking an empty street
on an autumn night right before it rains, and buddy holly my passion
        [a-down ta yau
        down ta yau
            a-down ta yau
but i'm living it now and ready to kick like a mantis with a half-eaten head in a
sex embrace, or big bopper with my hands over my head singing chantilly lace
all the way down.

leather & steel mesh in our flesh
& though we feel pain we're crash test dummies
telling america not to fuck up. it doesn't matter if we're bleeding
because steady sound makes us invincible.
i burst through birth & death dates like roadblocks
in *thunder road*. i see john wayne movies in my head
i ain't ever remembered seeing before. hey
nobody can stop the robot groove we're in
thundering steam engines pumping pit heads clear of water,
Bogomils bruising air non-stop howl. mop-head drummer
clacking galvanized sticks & man they've gotta chain
twisted through the GOD MACHINE
&'re sawing links through splintery chinks make sounds
of general dynamics blown to hell by iranian fanatics
while dudes thrash leathery brains free of bone. destroy the GOD MACHINE,
BEAT IT TO DEATH WITH HAMMERS,
TOSS TINNY FLESH TO BOARDS. we mash it against the wall
roll & howl in communion with every berserker
who ever jack-stepped across the planet.
and i want the Bogomils to keep up their thrash

wants those drunks at the bar to sit elbows in air
until the sun explodes into a supernova and we all become
glowing bits of t & a

but it ends
but it (keep it cool man) ends
but it ends.

& she sez it's the spiderz in the bed
& her grandmother talks to her through a hole in the wall
& to take it easy
& don't puke on the floor
she pops her kit & finds the tenderest vein

& i'm tired. & here's the alphabet; go make your own poem while i sleep:
ABCDEFGHIJKLMNOPQRSTUVWXYZ.
(later that same day): A & B & C & D & E & F & G & H & I & J & K &
L & M & N & O & P & Q & R & S & T & U & V & W & X & Y & Z.

i finally made it home through the snow drifts. dog was standing upright at the
end of his chain—twenty million years of evolution speeded up by his bondage.
he choked on his tongue; he howled gibberish at the shadow of my hand. "bad
dog, mad dog," i said. slather was frozen in a mask of canine tragedy; slather
was froth of december; slather was the ability of that dog's body to withstand
extremes of temperature. at least that's what i had read. i dusted off a fallen
branch. snow scattered like micro-chickens. threw it at dog. no yelp. then i
understood, though i still didn't believe him. ABCDE-
FGHIJKLMNOPQRSTUV & W. a fire engine flew by, the men clinging to
her back like tree toads. the moon was nowhere to be seen. (where was Legion)
i won't tell you about the wind. i refuse to tell you the number of cars that
climbed and turned in the purple distance. or the number of their headlights,
or of the existence of their implied wheels, and the number of times those
wheels turned necessarily or unnecessarily on the ice-covered road to drive car
X from point (guess) to point (guess again). i won't tell you that a rock, or a
fern, or a tree is writing this section, because i would be lying. and i am not just
freely associating at the typewriter. je est un autre. i am totally alone. dig?
ABCDEFGHIJKLMNOP, and on to infinity the dog of alphabets... would

not, could not, speak. instead it stood at the end of its chain and watched me with a supernal intelligence. i quake yet when i think of it. the nobility of its head. our domesticated series of signs still has the wolf in it, and i cannot master it, cannot call out to that snarl in the darkness with a little piece of potted meat in my hand. i might reach out with confidence and draw a blood-spouting stump back. but Legion's trapped inside this sentence kneeling forever on the bathroom floor in Big Boy's on Wisconsin Ave, surrounded by dirty cotton an inch of steel half in half outta her left arm, & if she reads this she'll know i love her. & when she knocks her head against these written walls you'll hear.

Seth's Pillar

I admire the serial martyrdom of the birds
& how the spring gnats scribble the face of the sun slate.

I love an old man's hand recalled in rainy weather
moving from nose to throat to solar plexus & returning
thin & liver spotted, to begin again.

I love a screw twisted through a lead plate after nightfall
despite a chorus of children's voices raised in protest.

& a sky tissued with rebel angels
& the final turnings of a copper coil
in a motor built by sweethearts & abandoned in tall grass.

the song-torn mouth propped on emptiness
praises the manifold, wind-blown, reticulated
breathings of lap-dogs & dray-horses decomposing
as Ur, Thebes, & Ninevah decomposed. the scutal
reptile skin of the monument flaking under
hammer blows of frost & thunder
sculpting the subtle thought per the scibile
is a subject fit for the shiftings of this prosody,

for can't we remember a better time? a pale woman
on a beach adding rows of numbers in her head
just to delight us? we found a horse shoe crab
half-buried in the sand. it brought glad tidings
from an opaque world of amethyst and amber.
an osprey sliced a wave. you pointed it out,
called it brother or sister (I forget which).
one cyclic claw yanked a fish to the sun.
one drop of sea from a cloudy fin colonized
the flat of your hand. you thought it sudden omen,
abrupt talisman. you were careful to guard this

"hint of immortality in the girl-scented beach house"
till the wind reclaimed it. then we dug
into clay and witnessed bone turning to elegant
stone, while dog-like reptiles frolicked
in the surf. like us they moved vital
limbs in joy. like us they never saw
the sword flash above the mauve horizon.
gravity was somehow gentler then. objects
never fell when dropped, but scratched
like roses at our finger tips. we gladly knelt
upon an aztec block as if to tempt
the aleatory gods, but knife & mallet turned
to scrolls incised with the nib of inexorable
law. & all that night the glittering pistons
of the moon moved the metaphysical carousel,
as each zodiacal mount, skewered on a twizzle stick
carried a thoughtful muse, her knuckles on her brow.

I admire a trivial machine twined among the glands,
the eloquence of empty jars in storm,
the little slit of nothing in a python's eye
gliding across a mud flat on a monkey-mad morning

& sleepless people propped side by side
lifting their voices together to protest
leather flames, pseudo-memories, one-winged butterflies
taped to computer chips, curious lights that wobble
before they fade. they sing, our loves destroy us
but we do not complain
more than a crow coughing
in a winter tree,
more than a headless sphinx
found in a midden heap. they say:

the stag's back with its load of arrows shot from an ineluctable bow
is plainly visible to us from where we sit

here in the portico of our vast hall; as is the stricken boar
laboring in the shadow of an oak, the spear's
handle translating each gasp into a dial-like regularity,
the barbed head sunk like an idol in the gut
waiting for the erosion of all flesh to disencumber it
of things secondary to its utility. we sit yawning or singing
at our tables, ready to hear gossip or story; ready
to embrace a new faith for the sake of novelty
or rediscover an old, while alien engines
arc in twilight hurling stony questions at the sky
that in turn become unasked for answers battering the masonry away
as we howl songs of the Golden Age while cracking
long bones for marrow, skulls for the a priori.

I love a black sphere reflected in gray water,
a giant figure screaming in the dark;
the buried mirror
uncovered by the tide
now reflecting a heaven of gulls after centuries.

Man Without Air

No longer a young man, I
trudge the tarmac, my son in my arms
behind his eyes a crystal taken from the head
of a hawk
with one knife thrust/
a twist & a pull
luminous point
pressed to his mother's belly
as she gave him to the dawn (2 Monads
        dividing
        in
        vagitus
        tumbling apart
        now
        speeding into the void)

  that crystal—AZOTH—glows in his brain
    the clean intelligence
  frozen in flight like an osprey
      in a
        block of ice.

It's so hard to walk the grid Descartes plotted
in delerium/
nothing to hold me to the earth
but the weight
of my desire.

Future/past   square within square &
circle within circle
    convince me
that beyond the earth's curve
is a wedding
of sun & moon
the Golden Animal
in dance

mounts
the Silver
fits perfectly

until they are through:
jazz in the night
Angel Midnight
stops judgement. No
Satan
riffling thunder
like a deck of cards
but a feast
we are invited to/
                    catch the dark garter
father mother
son & daughter

no christ wiping
bloody
handprints on the wedding
            dress
        no thumbprints of aboriginal
                    blood on the
                    invitation
but we, in perfect silence,
ingest the body
of the alphabet.

   Walking
in rain
over a hidden
desert

blooming prickly pear &
cacti become Wide and Soft embracing
                    Angels
with faces like shoe leather
tears of clear, bright stone

I stop, let
my son stand
in my shadow
he is afraid
trembling underlip
until he steps
into sunlight
hears a crow
call 3 X / now he

hurries
to the Angels
they surround him
whispering
the News.

It is as if a man could keep going without
                        breathing air
could build a world/fit it in a trunk/bury the trunk in
                        the side of a Mountain/
& when the trunk's uncovered & unhasped
unborn generations would see
a light filled treasure,
no crystal skull of dark inversions/ clattering of sinful
teeth
but a tree
that is a dead man's arm, each thew, each
sinew moved by a separate breeze
each breeze a thrumming wire nailed
to an angle inside the trunk

a village beneath the tree, huts
the color of dust,
& dolls hung by their chests
from thongs & hooks.

All visions
distilled in the fire
of future times
(hot war burning the guts
of the Great Man)
into this diorama: the original American
                              Testament
invisible hands
will not let this world be taken
as a museum piece/
        the dolls cry without mouths
            to the Watchers in their towers

while the man who keeps going without breathing
                            air
                    could tunnel
out the other side of the world
perhaps bathe his forehead
in cool rain
but chooses instead to rumble under
the shopping malls
tip the sidewalks
at crazy angles
rattle the diamond panes
of mortician's windows
shake skyscrapers like accusing fingers
at the clouds, saying:

"If you could count my words on your pulses
if you could sing these words
to passersby who shield their eyes
from your face with dark glasses
if you could walk with your children
in the city
yet know the earth stretches out all
around you
if you could sit all day in the heat

without a job
without hope
& without bitterness
if you could stand on the top of a cliff
without leaping off
with the 7 devils inside you
but teach those devils
to carry you through the air
to Quetzalcoatl's side
if you could catch rainwater
in a jar & watch
the land precipitate
from the water
the water become air
& tender worms
graze
on fungi
like the beasts
of the Peaceable Kingdom
& know that one
shake of your wrist
could send it all
back to chaos
yet resist that
movement
then a New World
will come, perhaps
& all things will remain
yet all things will be changed."

I am the Man without Air.
I hold my son close
& Look into his eyes.
What I see there ends this vision.

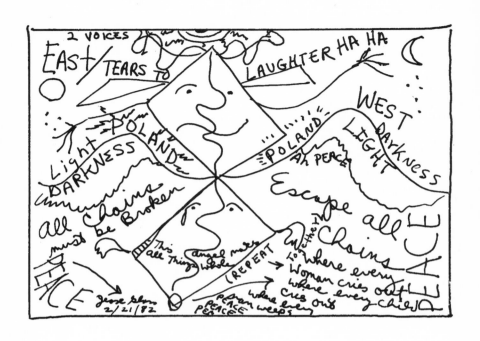

Peace Angel
Sound Text For 2 Voices
Peace For Poland

2 voices read & improvise.
1 Voice is East.
1 Voice is West.
Change & Repeat daily.

Poland Hears
(For Piotr Rypson)

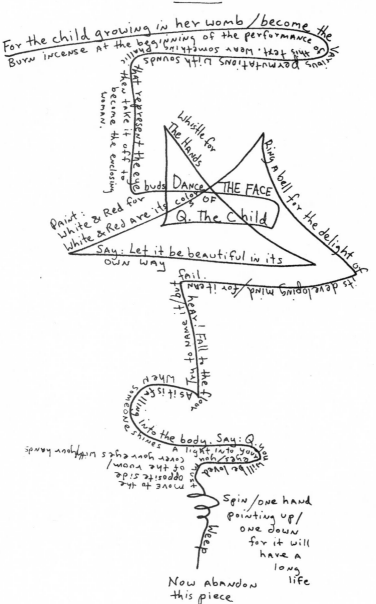

For the child growing in her womb / become the
Burn incense at the beginning of the performance of
this text. Wear something phallic.
various permutations. Light sounds
that represent the eye
then take it off to
become the enclosing
woman.

Whistle for The Hands

Ring a bell for the delight of

buds Dance THE FACE OF
Q. The Child

Paint: White & Red for
White & Red are its colors

Say: Let it be beautiful in its
own way

its developing mind / for it can
fail.
hear. I fall to the floor
to name it / but
As it is falling
when
someone shines
into the body. Say: Q.
A light into your eyes / you
will be loved
cover your eyes with your hands
move to the opposite side
of the room /
spray vinegar

Spin / one hand
pointing up /
one down
for it will
have a
long
life

Weep

Now abandon
this piece

To All Artists Dejection

Act out Obscurity & Hidden & Forgotten

The Dark Night Of The Soul

Suicide attempt

Gauguin's

You work sold by the Pound

A! I SUN you MAY Not SEE

Recovered
Uncovered
In the moldering
Stacks

Dismissed AS AN eccentric
Hide yr. face in yr. hands

For those working UNKNOWN
The jealous gods kill us: don't

laughed at some

too much.

Line up tombstones
Knock 'em down

shit-ass Job.
BRIGHT PROMISE

Re Cognition
End Less
Men tal
Bi rth
at Last

130

My Sculpture

The Distance between
Your Eye
& this page

Events for the Great Learning Orchestra (Stockholm)

Mirror Concert

Each member of the orchestra should choose a mirror (old or new, large or small, it is up to them) and use it for their score. Let them enter that mirror world of reversals and light and perform it for as long or as short a time as they'd like. The conductor should turn his back and lead while gazing at the orchestra by means of a small mirror held over his right (even days) or left (odd days) shoulder. The audience, too, should be seated with their backs to the orchestra and, during the performance, one or more small mirrors should be passed along so that the members of the audience can occasionally take a look at the orchestra as it plays, if they so choose. Ideally, this performance should take place while another orchestra is playing at exactly the same time in an adjoining room, but this is not absolutely necessary for the realization of the piece.

†

Seashell Event

Each member of the orchestra should find a seashell (preferably on a beach, but keepsakes, gifts, or purchases are acceptable), and should study the shell for a solid week or more so that they know every detail of the item. (If they begin to dream of the shell and its environment, it is a good sign that they have studied the shell sufficiently well.) Then the members of the orchestra should gather and improvise, using the shape, color, sound and texture of their shells as their score.

†

Sumi-e Event

A) The conductor takes a large sumi-e brush, dips it in black ink and paints a large square on a piece of heavy washi paper hung up so that the orchestra can clearly see the image. Then the orchestra "performs" the square for 10 minutes.

B) The conductor paints a triangle in the same manner on another piece of heavy washi paper and the orchestra performs the triangle for another 10 minutes.

C) The conductor paints a spiral in the same manner on another piece of heavy washi paper and the orchestra performs the spiral for another 10 minutes.

D) The conductor paints a circle in the same manner on another piece of heavy washi paper and the orchestra performs the circle for another 10 minutes.

E) The paintings of square, triangle, spiral, and circle are given to members of the audience.

End of concert.

†

Haiku Event

The orchestra plays together using a beat of five, then seven, then five. Five, seven, five. Five, seven, five. During the performance each player stops briefly to recite his or her favorite haiku against the orchestral background.

†

"As if" Event

Each member of the orchestra should play a standard piece of music as if they were a famous instrumentalist from the 19th, or earlier, centuries.

†

Fossil Print Piece

The conductor brings a large fossiliferous rock to the performance, inks it and makes impressions on paper from the stone by pressing the paper on the rock and rubbing the back of each page with a spoon or some other tool. The resulting prints (or frottage) should be handed out to the members of the orchestra, who will use the rubbings as their collective score.

Trope Event

1. I will read a moderately long poem. After I read each page I will destroy it in some ritualistic manner: tear it up, perhaps set it afire.

2. After the destruction is complete, I will pass out pencils and paper and ask the audience to write down—resurrect as it were, from the cooling ashes—what they recall of the content of the destroyed poem.

3. I will collect the papers from the audience and read the new text back to them. In this way the original text will be rescued from nothingness, & given a new body.

4. The life of the poem resides in the middle ground between trope & memory.

Jesse Glass
10/5/82
Milwaukee, Wisconsin.
4/23/2001
Urayasu, Japan.

Instant Camera Dance

Two dancers with instant cameras take photographs of each other as they move. The developing shots rain to the floor. The dancers toss the spent cameras to assistants who in turn toss freshly loaded cameras to the dancers so that the process may continue uninterrupted to the end of the piece. Photographs may be stepped upon by the dancers in order to help serendipity and chance processes along. After the event is finished the photographs will be arranged in a mosaic-like reconstruction of the dance. The visual component may be sold as one unit, or auctioned off shot by shot.

down
it came

down
from

the
autumn

sky

down
it came

down

& every-
one

rose

& wept
in the

city

(my
city)

& some
were
fly-
ing

& some
were
fall-
ing

& some
were
run-
ning

& some
were
burn-
ing

where
were

you
listen-
ing

watch-
ing

then?

in the
broken
earth?

in the
wounded
air?

in the
fractured
fire?

in the
shattered
sea?

where
were
you

listen-
ing

watch-
ing

then

when
every-
one

rose

& lookt
at the
sky

lookt
at the
sky

where
they
stood

in my
city

&
wept
?

Five

1.

cold light
edge
trees &

sidewalks w/
chalk
grackles thresh   July
lawns   6 A.M.
   voices
rough as
emery

   *

   these

2.

buildings
weave

their wickerwork   August
of heat around   6 A.M.
a song
a

3.

man smiles
from his window
      in T-shirt
looks out

at you

watching this   October
 sky   6 A.M.
 this
yellow invisible
   sun
   this
   word
flensed from the side
of syntax   is

4.

    buried in snow
  to keep turning
      one water   January
        bead   6 A.M.

one
  paper
tongue
    burning

  to

5.

speak   April
green   6 A.M.

The trowel-
jawed

armless
Jomon

clay
figurine

found
face-up

in a
rice-field

is my
love

watching
the sparkle

dirt
sky
sprout

root &
charcoal
glitter

ghost, if you
see buddha,
tell the butterfly

                    crow caws three times view of nine mountains

               one shoe to go—
               the blacksmith
               crimps a nail

A/a

Moon in a mirror
crushed beneath pneumatic hammers.
From its center   hound-like light
speeds beyond our walls

drags a radiant chain
along the earth.

A restless (   ) in a rusted [   ].

(Time out/
                    the sound
of tambourines/
blab of wet mouths/
gunning engines)

—"hear[d] a voice, as if
baskets & earthen pots were thrown
from place to place..."

A music quiet & complete
as the opening of frozen fingers.

***

Stone eyes peer back
a shovel-full
of liquid earth   swings
skyward

                    god-ocide
happened here: viz
cracked brows in ditches
oracle bones & a few
daggered dogs.

"Now I hear the falling of a block."

***

(Time out/
        the rnnnnt
of tuning forks/preamble
tines struck x times
in cheerless rooms
on bloodless wrists.

"There standeth one, at one of my ears,
and at another, another, howling like dogs;
and [I] said, ah you beggars!"

        a top springs
        2 inches
        into heaven.

A restless (coffin) in a rusted [   ].

        A certain hardening
        of fluid thought
        into dogma
        & large blocks
                of meaning
        Xed out

        w/some
        obscenity
        scrawled
        in penciled
        margins

& when the bag was opened an old man wide
of forehead & naked as a babe tumbled upon

the dirty floor. because of the emaciated
condition of the body, and its age, the workers
were given 2 guineas for their efforts by
the night attendant. so one "Wm. Blake"
came to the dissectionist's table.

[cage]

river the color of raw hands beneath the rain.

After Basho

Namu Amida Butsu

a ghost ejaculates at knifepoint in a bamboo grove

(season word: Tumor) any given truth

crashing through smoke

like a bombed wattle wall. Find

vast, brooding stains, carve

antiphonal structures

from them: carillons

inside a styrofoam cup

(smash zero zero X
end over end tumble)

stirrup bones stir: rumble
of frogs, mountain macaques

(season word: Open)

now

squat in silence

before a yellow cube

dent the perfect surface

with a small, clean hammer

tock! tock! tock! tock! tock!

        (b,o,u,n,d,l,e,s,s, c,o,m,p,a,s,s,i,o,n

where is that tea-stained skull?

Go Ha Ha Ha

Infinity the

size of a hen's egg
on little amber wheels

iron axles

regularly causes
gelastic seizures
completely beyond my control   that

"Laugh Is A Moral Laugh"
remains an enigma

to systematic justice. Me laugh?
Why, it's almost Painless

(likewise: you can
make me scream)

"You Don't Choose To Laugh"

constant laughter

laughing Center close to god
center close to verbal acuity
seat of Body/Mind

push the red button

seizure of Count Leo Tolstoi
ha. ha. ha.
into wife's open mouth
at train station

trepanning could stop it

eskimo's 11 types laughter
for each kind of snow

lasers melt snow

kicking bird, that name
i wonder if he ever laughed

face up in the river

carbines could cure it

stroke or tumor's
big cube of salt
knots up the thinkwaves

scissors remove it.

go ha ha ha
when they tell you to
go ha ha ha

In Ears of Crusted Flint

guns force a spanner
this eon's blemish
this vocal volley

graves of our ancestors
rotted w/city soot

what do those zeros say?
murder rotifera
cluster beneath one eye—
(bring out the microscope)

Buddha on sudden legs
occludes the nail-hole light
in ears of crusted flint
guns force a spanner

(What do those zeros say?
"murder rotifera")
Now we are building
Now we are tearing down

building the sightless machines
lifting the ladder of blades

m[   ]er w/knives of lead
m[   ]er w/knives of clay
m[   ]er w/knives of wood
m[   ]er w/knives of air

First the colossal legs
crumble in triplicate

roll the eyes right & left
then the stone lotuses

blossom a fever dream
render a rain of sand

see? we are building
see? we are tearing down

building the sightless machines
lifting the ladder of blades

Puppet Psalm I: Blokes On Film

Man is a phantom contained in a circle of steel. Agate & jade

spring-driven cogs

drive him relentlessly forward to Judgment.

He will strive to dance upon

hands powered by concealed counterbalances

at the 2nd, 3rd, & 4th gates

& he will contrive to cast an image of himself in lead

even at the 49th

& go upon rolling, transmigrative wheels assuming

varieties of pneuma & form from death to death

Tape (Robotic Voice):

Automaton, Marionette
  Blokes on film
   obey the force of the
upward pull
   as if thinking of Matter only;
however, on the one hand, we must agree
   such sentiments were not unknown to the ancient Shang
beyond the stage of the mechanical
   "Jumping lover"
who has "no moment to be merry."

Grotesque adjunct?
  glorified toys?

however, on the other hand, we must disagree
"...forcibly pulling & dragging them back..."
            vectors of power
Blokes on film
sleeping-sleeping-sleep
            sleep-etc.
& hopped-up prayers
            in cars by a highway
that few, or none, may cross & return to tell.

Voice:

in the stone called chaos Man will see a violin attacked by a lion

in the stone called guilt Man will see a woman's face

chewing the light away, (a calcite tumor

extends from her brow like an afterthought)

in the stone called blood Man will see a tattooed head in a box of salt, clean
            [as a wooden mallet
            at the bottom of a river

in the stone called stone Man will see a security camera filming his every move

Tape (Robotic Voice):

I know these things
for I have played the spy in the camp of Man
& have watched him grieve for a fortnight over lost vistas, & rise & exalt, mix-
            [ing zinc, bismuth,
& pyrite with an iridescent shovel.

Voice:

He remembers a ship which, with its steersman, went under water and did
[great damage to the enemy.

& He remembers a syphon used for quickly raising large quantities of water.

& He remembers a method that was used to lift weights by means of water and
[the above mentioned syphon.

& He remembers a method of constructing sluices where there is no fall of
[water, whereby ships can be raised to any required height within an
[hour or two.

& He remembers a machine that was driven by fire and ice.

& He remembers a drawbridge that was operated from within gates or walls.

& He remembers an air gun, a thousand of which were once discharged by the
[means of a single siphon.

& He remembers a musical instrument, with the airs marked on paper, which
[was played by one entirely unacquainted with music.

& He remembers a method of engraving on any kind of surface, by means of fire.

& He remembers a water horologue; which showed the motions of the heav-
[enly bodies by the flow of water.

& He remembers a carriage which contained various mechanical contrivances
[set in motion when the carriage was drawn by horses.

& He remembers a flying vehicle, or the possibility of being sustained in the
[air, and being conveyed through it.

& He remembers a method of conjecturing the desires and affections of dancers by analysis.

Tape (Robotic Voice):

& Man remembers new methods of constructing tensions and springs.

Puppet Psalm II: For Ventriloquist, Booming Chorus, & Percussion

Man's lens worthy of Spinoza

splits starlight
across his meat & bone

behind his ribs

a thickened nerve
called **Theosophy**
a tumor
called **Moonlight**
a lesion called
Origin, a tangle
of disruptions called
Ego, simply put

their purposeful maneuvering
THEIR PURPOSEFUL MANEUVERING
t,h,e,i,r p,u,r,p,o,s,e,f,u,l
m,a,n,e,u,v,e,r,i,n,g

the sound
a worm makes
in a nut

[Drum & Cymbals]

+

∗

+

*

+

*

stuff of teeth & pearls
burnt to lime
stanzas, slogans

clearly the work of a century of **slaves**

below the scaffolding war machines

practice by candle light
where mad monks live
(watch out!)
next to the sky

time to erase the proceedings
TIME TO ERASE THE PROCEEDINGS
t,i,m,e t,o, e,r,a,s,e t,h,e, p,r,o,c,e,e,d,i,n,g,s
Man spins on one fleshless foot

skull
ground down to a decimal point
frozen flowers could be turned
all directions
inside it

Selah.

Puppet Psalm III: Cantata for Puppet Coitus

Male & Female Voices:

YOU CAN HAVE ME ANYTIME YOU WANT ME, LOVE YA, X.
YOU CAN HAVE ME ANYTIME YOU WANT ME, LOVE YA, X.
YOU CAN HAVE ME ANYTIME YOU WANT ME, LOVE YA, X.
YOU CAN HAVE ME ANYTIME YOU WANT ME, LOVE YA, X.
YOU CAN HAVE ME ANYTIME YOU WANT ME, LOVE YA, X.
YOU CAN HAVE ME ANYTIME YOU WANT ME, LOVE YA, X.

Female Voice:

Don't talk to me in that tone of Voice.
Don't talk to me in that tone of Voice.
Don't talk to me in that tone of Voice.
Don't talk to me in that tone of Voice.
Don't talk to me in that tone of Voice.

Male Voice:

That guy musta eat nervous pills.
That guy musta eat nervous pills.
That guy musta eat nervous pills.
        The soul thrusts a wire through the flesh to animate this puppet of
            [gristle.

Male & Female Voices:

& IF THE DEAD TALK WHAT THEY SAY IS USELESS TO US NOW.
& IF THE DEAD TALK WHAT THEY SAY IS USELESS TO US NOW.
& IF THE DEAD TALK WHAT THEY SAY IS USELESS TO US NOW.
& IF THE DEAD TALK WHAT THEY SAY IS USELESS TO US NOW.
& IF THE DEAD TALK WHAT THEY SAY IS USELESS TO US NOW.
& IF THE DEAD TALK WHAT THEY SAY IS USELESS TO US NOW.

Female Voice:

& No more memories of muffled voices coming from the walls.
& No more memories of muffled voices coming from the walls.
& No more memories of muffled voices coming from the walls.

Male Voice:

To bind the black jaws of entropy.
To bind the black jaws of entropy.
To bind the black jaws of entropy.
      We see the fangs embedded in the bone.

[Tape (Robotic Voice) Repeats above as background to below.]

Male Voice:

"The winged corpse grips me
"w/ eagle talons
"& it grips me
"w/ the spurs of the flea
"in Karma Sutric embrace
"w/ a goat's jugular
"it grips me
"w/ the jaws of the candiru fish
"lodged in the urethra of a beautiful woman
"as she stands waist-deep & screaming in a muddy lagoon
"& it grapples itself
"to my broad, hod-carrier's shoulders
"my workman's skeletal system
"sways under the corpse's weight
"as the building I was in today swayed to the hidden earthquake whose epicenter
"was 400 miles away
"O corpse w/ the face of a man
"O corpse w/ the face of a woman
"one half visible to the eyes of the living

162

"the other visible to the eyes of the not-yet-born
"you grow bloated with the Mistral
"yr. skin is red as the worthless dirt of Carroll County
"yr. whistling mouth is crammed with ivory & slate
"yr. eyes distend from their sockets as you note, approvingly
"tomorrow's genocides, murders, and injustices
"yr. veins run black with Coca Cola
"& now each wing is a bayonet waving at the sky
"& now yr. gut is a swollen globe
"wrapped in parchment
"scrawled with anthropophagi & spouting Leviathans
"& I bend near to find America
"& I cannot

"though radiance
"awaits us

"transfigured bodies
"await us."

Tape (Robotic Voice):

"this is the voice of the torso in high weeds
"& this is the voice of a woman staring into her hands
"& this is the voice of a man who sleeps badly
"choking on all the hate he feels

"& I'm afraid says the torso in high weeds
"& I'm afraid says the woman staring into her hands
"& I'm afraid" says the man who sleeps badly
"of all the hate I feel"
"& I'm afraid says the girl w/ her face to the wall
"& I'm afraid says the wooden-eyed boy
"& I'm afraid says the idiot savant now popular in every concert hall
"& I'm afraid says the man whose heart is silting up

"that tomorrow
"is most definitely
"here—

"& there is nothing beyond the mud door
"& there is nothing beyond the stone door
"& there is nothing beyond the wooden door
"& there is nothing beyond the bronze door
"& there is nothing beyond the shimmering door of water
"& there is nothing beyond the raven-feather door
"& there is nothing beyond the door of living flesh
"& there is nothing beyond the door of lacquered flames
"& there is nothing
"& there is nothing
"& there is nothing."

e song

(for marton koppany)

brave

Txt

invites

an eye

to

thread

Our luminous fracture

long into

One

raptus

E

In The Realm Of The Mothers, A

Celestina Played by
Sugared Fingers

1.

Green ladies   What Do You Require?
(refusing to leave no matter
                the ritual)   heads tipped forward in sleep/ pierce
space w/ thin, pointed dreams   ecstatic journey
(sun & (moon & (number
these bricked-in humors a(n)/O(r)ther(n)(pr(es)ence) in their skins

snapping the death mask out & up

they continue to lick long hands in commentary.

2.

now eat
        this **a,s,t,o,n,i,s,h,i,n,g,f,r,a,g,m,e,n,t**

                Worked into tektite-stuccoed lozenges
                        by angelic foot & elbow
(immediate Gift, ya knaow,

swallow
this jagged, "spotless" sentence

"i 'ad 'ever/'een/'othing/'ike/ 't/ 'efore, ya knaow."

I// C/
UT
MY TH/
UMB
& THE B/
LOOD
R/
OLL/
S FORTH, FO/
R EVERY DARK/
ENING BEAD i DA/
MN Y/
O/
UR LI/
FE

....surely your

                             Eye

      spanned the lit
Miraculous
                  (BLADE (that is Metallschock, Miracle, Autumn & Outrage
so does language
      reduced to slivers,
      suspended from 14 strings

         stab
at itself
"with its cloak flying!"

"I am a friend of a friend
      5 things
      happen to me..."

10:45 a.m. it rains on a dying horse, steam rolling back from its skull like a blanket of lace/

it's time to sing

Sun-thickened ropes of syrup

of everything taken

in the backs of their throats

away=the null sign

we mull over

they sit in chairs

fat & greasy on the pane

of the eye, music

the earth cooling around them.

drawn back into resonant wire,

varnished wood

birds flashing thru each written forehead...urging the process on...

a song-torn mouth

propped on emptiness

dulcet 8-fold machine

so much like a body's dimpled chambers

opening on fluids & slumber, slumber & measure.

then walk to where young people lose themselves in contemplation of what may be:

a motorcycle gang

kicking hell out of something

metal in the lobby of an apartment

building 20 stories high

the leader cuts his hand

& delicate, feather-like marks fly upward from the mouths of everyone

"for you

a brace of unlimbered harmonies..."

Ladies, lean forward—

long time disburdened

of silence

skate a fingernail
over vitrified voids,
listen to angels scream.

my first thought, I have to admit, was Wow.

About the Author

Following in the Gage tradition, since receiving extensive damage to his frontal lobes as a young man working as a tire recapper, farrier's assistant, swipe and roustabout, Glass has exhibited himself at various colleges and universities since 1978.

His current show features Glass as a professor of Literature and History in the Graduate and Undergraduate programs at Meikai (Bright Sea) University in Chiba, Japan. His supporting cast includes his wife, Maya, his son Yoichi and his daughter Tennessee.

Look for Glass' work on Ubu Web, in the film *Faites vos Jeux* by Filmgruppe Chaos, in *Visiting Walt* from the University of Iowa Press, and in scads of literary magazines and websites devoted to the "sweet science."

His books include *Song for Arepo*, *Against the Agony of Matter*, *Make Death Die*, and studies of Maryland history and folklore. Glass' visual work is part of the Ruth and Marvin Sackner Archive for Visual Poetry, and his sound poetry collaborations are available from Rod Summers and Charles Krutzen.

Typeset in Adobe Garamond™, a digital interpretation of the roman types of Claude Garamond and the italic types of Robert Granjon, which capture the beauty and balance of the original Garamond typefaces. In the 16th Century, roman and italic were not intermixed and Granjon's italics have been adjusted somewhat to allow for intermixing. These are "authentic revivals" of the vraye parangonne specimens held at the Plantin-Moretus Museum in Antwerp, Belgium.

Designed by Daniel Sendecki

West House Books
http://www.westhousebooks.co.uk

Ahadada Books
http://www.ahadadabooks.com